The Marketing Manual

The Chartered Institute of Marketing/Butterworth-Heinemann Marketing Series is one of the most comprehensive, widely used and important collections of books in marketing and sales presently available worldwide. 4

As the CIM's official publisher Butterworth-Heinemann develops, produces and publishes all the titles in the series with and on behalf of the CIM. We aim to publish definitive marketing books for both students and practitioners that help them to achieve the highest possible standards in their marketing education and practice.

The student texts and books are written and developed by leading marketing educators and CIM senior examiners for those taking the Certificate, Advanced Certificate and Diploma courses. The titles for practitioners are from leading marketing experts and senior CIM members for use on vocational programmes and also to deliver the very latest marketing thinking and techniques to the busy executive.

The Chartered
Institute of Marketing

Formed in 1911, The Chartered Institute of Marketing is now the largest professional marketing management body in Europe with over 60,000 members located worldwide. Its primary objectives are focused on the development of awareness and understanding of marketing throughout UK industry and commerce and in the raising of standards of professionalism in the education, training and practice of this key business discipline.

Books in the series

Below-the-line Promotion, John Wilmshurst

The CIM Handbook of Export Marketing, Chris Noonan

The CIM Handbook of Selling and Sales Strategy, David Jobber

The CIM Handbook of Strategic Marketing, Colin Egan and Michael J. Thomas

CIM Marketing Dictionary (fifth edition), Norman A. Hart

Copywriting, Moi Ali

Creating Powerful Brands (second edition), Leslie de Chernatony and Malcolm McDonald

The Creative Marketer, Simon Majaro

The Customer Service Planner, Martin Christopher

Cybermarketing, Pauline Bickerton, Matthew Bickerton and Upkar Pardesi

The Effective Advertiser, Tom Brannan

Integrated Marketing Communications, Ian Linton and Kevin Morley

Key Account Management, Malcolm McDonald and Beth Rogers

Market-led Strategic Change (second edition), Nigel Piercy

The Marketing Book (third edition), Michael J. Baker

Marketing Logistics, Martin Christopher

Marketing Research for Managers (second edition), Sunny Crouch and Matthew Housden

The Marketing Manual, Michael J. Baker

The Marketing Planner, Malcolm McDonald

Marketing Planning for Services, Malcolm McDonald and Adrian Payne

Marketing Plans (third edition), Malcolm McDonald

Marketing Strategy (second edition), Paul Fifield

Practice of Advertising (fourth edition), Norman A. Hart

Practice of Public Relations (fourth edition), Sam Black

Profitable Product Management, Richard Collier

Relationship Marketing, Martin Christopher, Adrian Payne and David Ballantyne

Relationship Marketing for Competitive Advantage, Adrian Payne, Martin Christopher, Moira Clark and Helen Peck

Retail Marketing Plans, Malcolm McDonald and Christopher Tideman

Royal Mail Guide to Direct Mail for Small Businesses, Brian Thomas

Sales Management, Chris Noonan

Trade Marketing Strategies, Geoffrey Randall

Forthcoming

Relationship Marketing: Strategy and Implementation, Helen Peck, Adrian Payne, Martin Christopher and Moira Clark

Services Marketing, Colin Egan

The Marketing Manual

Michael J. Baker

Strathclyde Business School

Published on behalf of The Chartered Institute of Marketing

OXFORD   BOSTON   JOHANNESBURG   MELBOURNE   NEW DELHI   SINGAPORE

Butterworth-Heinemann
Linacre House, Jordan Hill, Oxford OX2 8DP
225 Wildwood Avenue, Woburn, MA 01801-2041
A division of Reed Educational and Professional Publishing Ltd

 A member of the Reed Elsevier plc group

First published 1998

© Michael J. Baker 1998

British Library Cataloguing in Publication Data
A catalogue record for this book is available from the British Library

ISBN 0 7506 3652 1

Composition by Genesis Typesetting, Rochester, Kent
Printed and bound in Great Britain

FOR EVERY TITLE THAT WE PUBLISH, BUTTERWORTH-HEINEMANN
WILL PAY FOR BTCV TO PLANT AND CARE FOR A TREE.

Contents

Preface

This book has been developed primarily for persons who are pursuing a formal course of study in marketing strategy and management at the advanced undergraduate or postgraduate level – a Master's in marketing, MBA or the postgraduate Diploma of The Chartered Institute of Marketing. It has three basic objectives:

1 To test the user's understanding of key concepts and practices.
2 To reinforce learning by applying the knowledge base to the solution of practical problems.
3 To develop skills and competences in problem solving and communication and, particularly, in the specification, diagnosis and solution of marketing problems.

The structure of the book follows the sequence adopted by most marketing management courses. It has been designed for use specifically with *The Marketing Book* (ed. Michael J. Baker, 3rd edition, 1994), *Marketing Strategy and Management* (Michael J. Baker, 2nd edition, 1992) and *Strategic Marketing Management* (Wilson and Gilligan, 2nd edition, 1997). However, its approach and content are directly relevant to other leading texts on the subject.

Each chapter in the book deals with a distinct phase or stage in the strategic marketing planning (SMP) process and so may be used as appropriate quite independently of the others. However, taken together, the chapters cover the complete process involved in developing a strategic marketing plan and so may be used by students for purposes of case analysis as well as by practitioners working on real-world problems. While the latter are not the primary target it is hoped that practitioners will find the various diagnostics and pro formas a useful *aide-mémoire* when developing practical marketing plans.

As is explained in greater detail in Chapter 1, the purpose of the book is to provide a framework to address the four fundamental questions facing the planner/decision maker:

- Where am I now?
- Where do I want to go?
- How do I get there?
- How will I know when I've arrived?

To answer these questions the book comprises eight chapters, each of which addresses a specific topic.

Chapters 1 and 2 provide a broad introduction to the structure of the book, the approach to be followed and a discussion of issues such as problem definition, data collection and analysis, etc. which are common to all problem solving.

Chapters 3 to 8 deal with discrete steps or phases involved in developing a comprehensive marketing plan and comprise narrative (to remind users of relevant concepts, ideas and techniques) and a series of assignments or exercises to test and apply their knowledge and understanding. Taken together, the worked exercises provide the essential elements of an operational marketing plan.

Chapter 1

Strategic marketing planning

Introduction

As noted in the Preface, the primary objective of this book is to reinforce understanding of the key concepts and ideas covered by formal courses in marketing strategy and management. Its content and structure will also be useful to practitioners as an *aide-mémoire* or checklist covering the basic steps involved in developing an operational marketing plan.

In this chapter we open with a short overview of the nature and purposes of strategic marketing planning (SMP) and a fuller statement of objectives. Next, we describe the structure of the book and the organizing principles which determined this. Specifically, we identify a number of key questions which the planner/decision maker must address and answer in developing an effective marketing strategy and plan for its implementation. Each of these key questions is the subject of a chapter which contains narrative, to remind the reader of salient issues and topics, and a series of exercises or assignments which require application of knowledge (and experience) to produce a useful solution.

Having described the structure and sequence to be followed, we conclude with some advice on how to use the book to best effect. This includes completion of the exercises themselves, interpretation of the answers provided, and the role of the Barnstaple Company case study as an example of the implementation of the exercises to produce a new strategy and operational marketing plan for a small company experiencing declining profitability.

Strategic marketing planning (SMP)

As noted in *Marketing Strategy and Management* (Baker, 1992), there is no single, universally accepted definition of SMP. Seven definitions identified by Brownlie (1983) in a survey of the subject are cited:

1 The answers to two questions implicit in Drucker's early conceptualization of an organization's strategy: 'What is our business? And what should it be?'
2 Chandler defined strategy as: 'the determination of the basic long-term goals and objectives of an enterprise, and the adoption of courses of action and the allocation of resources necessary for carrying out these goals'.
3 Andrews' definition of strategy combines the ideas of Drucker and Chandler: 'Strategy is the pattern of objectives, purposes or goals and plans for achieving these goals, stated in such a way as to define what business the company is in or is to be in and the kind of company it is or is to be'.
4 Hofer and Schendel define an organization's strategy as: 'the fundamental pattern of present and planned resource deployments and environmental interactions that indicates how the organization will achieve its objectives'.
5 According to Abell, strategic planning involves: 'the management of any business unit in the dual tasks of anticipating and responding to changes which affect the marketplace for their products'.
6 In 1979, Derek Wynne-Jones, head of the planning and strategy division of P.A. Management Consultants, considered that strategic planning: 'embraced the overall objective of an organization in defining its strategy and preparing and subsequently implementing its detailed plans'.
7 Christopher Lorenz, late editor of the management page of the *Financial Times*, considered strategic planning to be: 'the process by which top and senior executives decide, direct, delegate and control the generation and allocation of resources within a company'.

But, while these definitions may differ in the particular, there does appear to be a common thread, which is that SMP is concerned with establishing the goal or purpose of an organization and the means chosen for achieving that goal. Perhaps, then, the differences of opinion revolve around how one defines an organization or 'business'. We must recognize that differences of size, scale, diversity, complexity, etc. will inevitably result in significant differences between 'firms' and so make generalizations about them difficult if not impossible. To overcome or reduce this difficulty most analysts now prefer to define the business in terms of its strategic functions rather than try to define businesses first and then discover that there are major discrepancies in strategic functions between them. As a consequence, most discussions of SMP are now focused upon the concept of the strategic business unit (SBU) which has been defined succinctly by Arthur D. Little as:

> A Strategic Business Unit – or Strategy Centre – is a business area
> with an external market place for goods and services, for which
> management can determine objectives and execute strategies
> independent of other business areas. It is a business that could
> probably stand alone if divested. Strategic Business Units are the
> 'natural' or homogeneous business of a corporation.

Arthur D. Little's reference to the 'divestment' of a business provides an important clue to the approach followed by most major management texts – an approach which often makes such books appear largely irrelevant to the average manager. Unless targeted at the small- to medium-sized enterprise (SME) books dealing with strategy and planning almost invariably assume they are dealing with a multinational corporation competing globally through a portfolio of divisions (SBUs) each of which is addressing a distinct market. In reality, in most advanced economies over ninety per cent of persons are employed in SMEs with fewer than 200 employees. They work for an SBU!

The point we are seeking to make is that the formulation of strategy and the development of action plans is relevant to all sizes and types of organization. Obviously, large multinational and multidivisional firms such as General Motors, IBM or Unilever will face much greater complexity than small firms with a single product line serving a local or regional market. In crafting a strategy and putting it into practice complex organizations will need to perform much more elaborate evaluations than will simple ones. None the less, the same approach and procedures apply to all. In order to cater for this diversity the book follows the approach of the major texts and provides diagnostics and advice appropriate to the large firm. It is hoped that the case study (Barnstaple Company) chosen to exemplify the application of the recommended techniques and procedures will make clear that these are just as relevant to an SME but that such firms will need to be selective in deciding what is appropriate for them.

During the second half of this century attitudes towards strategic planning have gradually evolved from closely prescribed, centrally controlled systems planning approaches to much more open-ended, broadly based methods involving wide participation. In the process much criticism has been levelled against the value of SMP. Perhaps the most influential critic has been Henry Minztberg, who takes the view that strategies 'emerge' as managers react to events and contingencies that confront them. Few practising managers would disagree that much strategy is formulated in this way but most would reject the conclusion that this negates the relevance or importance of formal strategic planning of the kind advocated in the book. Briefly put, if you have no formal strategy and plans for achieving it, how can you know that changing conditions call for a change in direction and know what to do next?

As Montaigne, the French essayist, expressed it:

> No wind blows in favour of the ship with no port of destination.

In the modern idiom Levitt expressed exactly the same thought when he said:

> If you don't know where you are going any road will take you there.

This book takes the view that as a result of accelerating technological change, of global competition and the dynamic and often turbulent markets that have resulted, the need for a structured approach to problem solving has never been greater. That said, the techniques and methods proposed are intended to provide a framework, not a blueprint. It is up to you, the decision maker, to decide how important any given stage or activity is, and to allocate time and resources accordingly.

Objectives

> There is a tide in the affairs of men which, if taken at the flood,
> leads on to fortune.

In an increasingly sophisticated, complex and technological world it is not difficult to overlook the simple fact that whereas the *kind* of problems decision makers are called on to solve may have changed, their essential *nature* has not. Problems have always existed and decision makers have always been faced with imperfect information, uncertainty and constraints on time and other resources which would be helpful to the solution of their problem. On the basis that people should learn from experience – which, over time, becomes codified as knowledge – it follows that they should seek to apply past lessons to current problems. Consideration of the manner in which earlier decision makers have addressed and solved particular problems suggests that problems may usefully be classified in terms of their nature and useful generalizations derived concerning their solution. Such generalizations provide analytical frameworks and classification systems which offer the opportunity to impose structure on complex problems and help to identify the courses of action open to the decision maker. In doing so they ensure that the limited resources available can be focused directly on the key issues and so enhance the likelihood of an acceptable solution.

Faced with a problem, it may be assumed to be similar in kind to problems encountered in the past and a previously successful solution can then be applied. Often such an approach will work, especially if assumptions are made on the basis of a careful analysis and diagnosis which shows that there are sufficient similarities between the present and prior problems for there to be a strong likelihood that the previously successful solution will work. In the physical sciences, where the properties of objects and their interactions and interrelationships can be clearly established (the laws of science), it can reasonably be expected that if an experiment is replicated (addresses the same problem again) then the outcome will always be the same.

Unfortunately, in the social sciences, and particularly in the case of the synthetic multi-disciplinary business and management subjects such as marketing, it is almost impossible to hold constant the properties of the objects of an 'experiment' to be certain of an outcome. Thus, when considering the essence of marketing – the act of exchange between a seller and a buyer – it is almost impossible to replicate precisely one sale with another. Sellers may control the specification of their product, its sale and delivery very closely but every buyer will differ in some degree from every other. In practice this may not be significant because for most products and services an exact match is not essential and there will be a sufficient number of buyers with similar, albeit marginally different needs, to constitute a viable market (segment).

But, in marketing, the fundamental problem is not one of completing a transaction between a buyer and a seller – important though this may be – it is one of establishing a continuing relationship between them. Whereas one-off sales may be profitable in their own right, all the evidence points to the fact that it costs much more to create a customer than to keep one (rule-of-thumb estimates put the ratio at 5:1). It follows that sellers hope to establish a continuing relationship with their customers which will predispose them to repurchase from the same seller, when they have a need for fresh supplies of the product in question.

A simple approach to evaluating the relationship between buyer and seller is the Buy-Grid analytic framework developed by Robinson, Farris and Wind (1967) illustrated in Figure 1.1.

As with many of the diagnostic/analytical tools used in the book, a complex subject has been reduced to two basic dimensions – Buy Phases and Buy Classes.

The eight Buy Phases summarize the stages the buyer *may* go through from identifying a consumption need to satisfying it. We say 'may' because the identification of Buy Classes is based on the observation that buyers are only likely to complete each of the stages in the sequence when faced with a new buy. As we describe below, if the prospective buyer has some (modified rebuy) or extensive experience (straight rebuy) of the object they may omit many of the stages.

For commonplace and frequently purchased consumer convenience goods such as foodstuffs, cooking oil, detergents, etc. the importance of repeat purchasing and 'brand' loyalty is obvious. Further, because the elapsed time between one purchase and the next is relatively short, much of this purchasing becomes habitual and a form of routinized problem solving. While consumers may be willing to consider alternative purchases, by and large they will tend to stick with the products whose performance is known to give acceptable levels of satisfaction. To do otherwise would be to waste time which could be put to other more satisfying uses.

BUY CLASSES

		New buy	Modified rebuy	Straight rebuy
B U Y	1 Anticipation or recognition of a problem (need) and a general solution			
	2 Determination of characteristics and quantity of needed item			
	3 Description of characteristics and quantity of needed item			
	4 Search for and qualification of potential sources			
P H A S E S	5 Acquisition and analysis of proposals			
	6 Evaluation of proposals and selection of supplier(s)			
	7 Selection of an order routine			
	8 Performance feedback and evaluation			

Source: Robinson *et al.* (1967). *Industrial Buying and Creative Marketing*. Allyn & Bacon.

Figure 1.1 The buy-grid analytic framework for industrial buying situations

It is because consumer convenience goods have a generally low salience for consumers and because they are purchased frequently that changes in both supply and demand tend to be almost imperceptible. Cumulatively and over time changes may be considered, as concern over dietary factors and their association with disease and morbidity makes clear, but, as a working generalization, competition in such markets tends to focus on the tactical manipulation of the marketing mix in essentially stable markets. (These observations apply equally to frequently purchased industrial products such as raw materials, fabricated materials and supplies.)

This does not mean that firms selling frequently purchased products and services do not have a need for strategic planning – they do – but it does mean that they are more likely to emphasize short-term tactical planning and see long-term strategic planning as a cumulation of such short-term plans. This contrasts significantly with the situation in industries where repurchase cycles may be anything from 3–4 to 15–20 or more years. Over periods of this length it is likely that substantial innovation and change will have occurred, so that not only will the array of products and services available to the customer have changed but so will the customer's expectations. While customers may have been satisfied with the performance of the product that they now need to replace, and so be willing to consider repurchasing from the same source, they will be unlikely to do so without establishing what else is available, which may offer greater satisfaction for any given expenditure. In other words, both problem and possible solution may have changed and some re-evaluation is called for. The *kind* of problem has changed but its *nature* has not.

Firms operating in markets with extended repurchase cycles clearly need to look much further ahead in their planning and so give at least equal emphasis to strategy as tactics. To begin with, they need to consider the value in use derived by the customer over the lifetime of the product and the kinds of service which may be necessary to ensure continuing high performance and satisfaction. Such service needs provide the opportunity for a continuing relationship between buyer and seller so that the seller should be the first to know when repurchase is likely to occur and what the customer's needs and expectations are likely to be. It follows that the strategic and tactical planning cycles for firms manufacturing and selling durable products – both industrial and consumer – should be geared to the expected repurchase cycle.

Of course, repurchase cycles are not the sole consideration – old consumers exit markets and new consumers enter them continuously. New customers present both the greatest opportunity and the greatest challenge. New customers may become customers for life. But new customers may not become customers at all but lost to your competitors. New customers entering a market for the first time are faced with the most complex problem-solving situation, for they have all the existing alternatives available for consideration. In the absence of any direct prior experience their problem solving is likely to be both more thorough and more extended than is the case with repurchase decisions. Firms seeking to win new customers will need to develop specific strategies and tactics for doing so.

The purpose of this book is to help the student/manager address the critical task of relating the body of knowledge (distilled experience) contained in marketing textbooks and journals to the solution of real-world problems. To do this effectively one must decide first what is the nature of the problem to be addressed and then be able to select the most appropriate solution. Inevitably some individuals will have a greater aptitude for diagnosis and prognosis than others but the fact that our medical schools graduate large numbers of doctors every year with sufficient skills should reassure us that managerial problem-solving skills can be learned and improved with practice. This book is seen as a contribution to this process of both learning and improving skills.

Structure and sequence

The organizing principle of the book is that the business planner/decision maker is faced with four fundamental questions:

- Where am I now?
- Where do I want to go?
- How do I get there?
- How will I know when I've arrived?

In turn, each of these fundamental questions can be disaggregated into a series of more focused subquestions which, together, provide a framework for comprehensive analysis. For example Wilson and Gilligan's book is organized around the framework shown in Figure 1.2, while Doyle proposes the sequence set out in Figure 1.3.

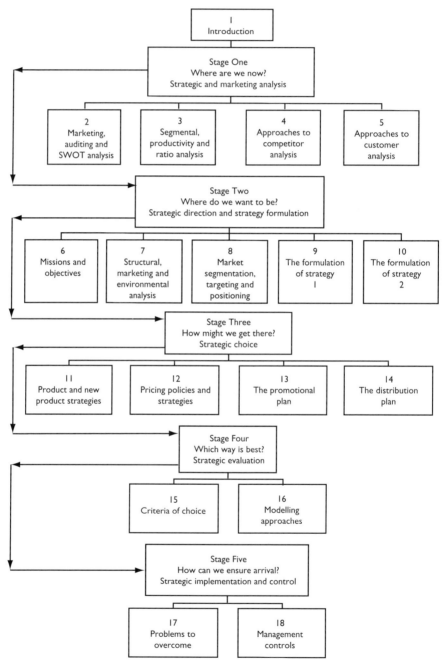

Figure 1.2 Wilson and Gilligan's components of a marketing strategy

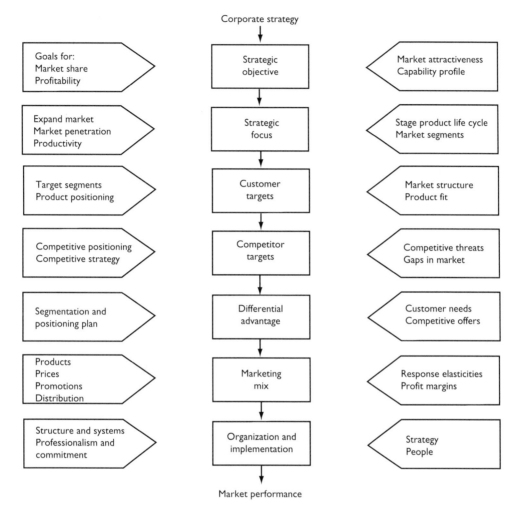

Figure 1.3 Doyle's components of a marketing strategy

The sequence/structure we propose contains elements of both these frameworks but is based essentially on our four fundamental questions, as can be seen from Figure 1.4.

Before seeking to address these issues in the particular there are two general topics which deserve attention first.

1 What is marketing and a marketing orientation?
2 What factors appear to determine competitive success?

By combining these questions with those set out in Figure 1.4 we have identified ten discrete steps or stages, as illustrated in Figure 1.5, and it is these which provide the structure of the book as a whole and the content of Chapters 3 to 8 inclusive.

Key question	Analytic step	Issue addressed
1 Where am I now?	Diagnosis	Where is the company now and why?
2 Where do I want to go?	Prognosis	Where is the company headed?
	Objectives	Where should the company be headed?
3 How do I get there?	Strategy	What options are available? Which should I choose?
	Tactics	What specific actions should be taken by whom, when?
4 How will I know when I've arrived?	Feedback and control	What measures should be watched to establish performance?

Figure 1.4 Framework for a marketing strategy

Question	Analytic step	Stage/section
Where am I now?	Diagnosis	1 How marketing orientated are you? What business are you in?
		2 Marketing and competitive success – a review of critical success factors
Where do I want to go?	Prognosis	3 Marketing appreciation – where are we now and what does the future hold in store for us?
		4 Conclusions and key assumptions
		5 Objectives – where do we want to go?
	Objectives	6 Market segmentation
How do I get there?	Strategy	7 Core strategy – what approach shall we take?
	Tactics	8 Turning ideas into action – devising the marketing mix; selecting key policies
		9 Developing the marketing plan
How will I know when I've arrived?	Control	10 How will we know when we've arrived? – measurement, feedback and control

Figure 1.5 Ten stages

Using the book

In Figure 1.5 we have identified ten stages or steps involved in the SMP process which conform closely with what is often termed the 'normative' theory. Unfortunately, 'theory' is often regarded as distinct from and, sometimes, diametrically opposed to 'practice'. We say 'unfortunately' because the essence of a normative theory is that it should mirror best practice – the two are inextricably linked. Normative theories are essentially *deductive* in the sense that one develops particular recommendations derived from many observations of practice. Clearly, this is quite different from a theory based on *induction*, where one generalizes from the particular to the general. I observe that the XYZ company was successful so I theorize that all other companies will succeed if they copy XYZ's approach. Only repeated observations can confirm if this is a reasonable hypothesis to draw.

Textbooks and formal courses reflect the current consensus of what is known about a subject – the knowledge base. The most efficient and effective way of communicating this is through education and it is for this reason that there are only minor differences in the structure and content of books such as this – it represents both academics' and practitioners' views of the approach to SMP. Having said this, it is necessary to repeat the warning that this is a framework, not a blueprint.

A structured and formalized approach to SMP offers guidance on what *may* need to be done, not what *has* to be done. The relevance and importance of each step and the time and effort devoted to it will depend on the experience and needs of the planners in the context of the specific problem they are seeking to solve. The framework should not inhibit creativity or innovativeness – it is intended to provide direction and discipline to harness these qualities and ensure high levels of performance. Each exercise has been designed to achieve these ends.

Each exercise is preceded by its own short introduction which explains its purpose and the procedures to be followed in completing it. To assist in the interpretation of your own solutions we have provided 'answers' or commentary based on research or other evidence related to the issue. We would remind you that there are few, if any, 'right' answers, especially when concerned with competitive behaviour. Accordingly, while some alternatives or courses of action may seem 'better' than others the object of the exercise is to determine what you do or propose to do. If you cherry-pick what you think the 'textbook' answer is rather than your genuine belief or opinion, you are likely to gain little from completing the exercises.

As a workbook the intention is that you should write your answers down in the book as you complete each checklist, scale, matrix or whatever. We stress that the space provided *does not* reflect any perception of the importance of each exercise. In some cases there will be more than enough room for your answers. In other cases, where a topic is particularly relevant, complex or important for you and your organization, you will want to use supplementary sheets. Do so.

Finally, as an appendix to this chapter, we have included a short case study concerning the Barnstaple Company. This is a deceptively simple problem – the company manufactures diaries, has an unsold inventory which is now practically worthless and has sustained a loss for the third year in a row. What should the new CEO do? At the end of each chapter, to exemplify the use of the various techniques and procedures we will relate these to the Barnstaple Company to illustrate their practical application.

Summary

In this chapter we have argued that a formal approach to SMP is desirable and will lead to improved performance. A preferred structure and sequence have been proposed which identify a series of key questions which need to be addressed. These and the exercises to answer these key questions may be summarized as:

1	**Question:**	What is marketing and a marketing orientation? How does this differ from other business orientations?
	Exercise 3.1	What business are we in?
	Exercise 3.2	How marketing orientated are you?
2	**Question:**	What contribution does marketing make to competitive success?
	Exercise 4.1	Competitive critical success factors
3	**Question:**	Where are we now and what does the future hold in store for us? (The marketing appreciation)
	Exercise 5.1	PEST analysis
	Exercise 5.2	Cross-impact matrix
	Exercise 5.3	Completing the ETOM
	Exercise 5.4	Critical success factors
	Exercise 5.5	Skills and competences
	Exercise 5.6	Objective needs analysis
	Exercise 5.7	Macroenvironmental threat and opportunity matrix
	Exercise 5.8	Task environment threat and opportunity matrix
	Exercise 5.9	Occurrence/impact matrix
	Exercise 5.10	SWOT analysis
4	**Question:**	Where do we want to go?
	Exercise 6.1	The product demand curve
	Exercise 6.2	The product life cycle curve
	Exercise 6.3	Ansoff's growth/vector matrix
	Exercise 6.4	The directional policy matrix (DPM)
	Exercise 6.5	The Boston box

But, first, we need to review some general issues involved with problem solving and decision making and these form the subject of the next chapter.

Appendix: The Barnstaple Company

(This case study is an updated version of an original case study of the Harvard Business School (ICH DC2P6) of the same name.)

Mr James Barnstaple Jr, the newly appointed general manager of the Barnstaple Company, in January 1993 called a conference of the company's production manager, sales manager, and accountant. The subject of discussion was an inventory of diaries manufactured in 1992 at a cost of £250,000 which, having become obsolete, was practically valueless.

The Barnstaple Company

The Barnstaple Company was a long-established manufacturer of a nationally known line of diaries. For many years the enterprise had been profitable, but since the death of Mr James Barnstaple Sr, in 1989, profits had steadily declined. Operations in 1991 and 1992 had resulted in substantial losses. Ownership of the company had passed to Mr Barnstaple's widow, who had entrusted active management of the business to his assistants, responsibility being vested in the accountant.

Mr James Barnstaple Jr went to work in the Barnstaple Company office immediately after his graduation in June 1991. He rapidly became familiar with the company's operations, its policies, and its problems, and on 1 January 1993 he assumed full charge of the business under the title of general manager.

The line of diaries manufactured by the Barnstaple Company included about 300 items. Single diaries were sold direct to individuals by means of magazine advertising. Banks and similar commercial enterprises purchased diaries in lots of 500 or more and used them for advertising purposes. College stores and student associations bought larger quantities of special designs, dated from August to the following August, for distributing to purchasers of memberships at the beginning of the academic year.[1] The retail trade was supplied largely through jobbers. Sales of different items in the line varied from 200 to 300,000 units a year. Business was extremely seasonal, and inventory carried after 1 January became practically valueless.

Four-fifths of the 1992 sales were of 200 staple items that varied little in design from year to year. The remaining one-fifth was equally divided between a group of 100 novelty styles which were frequently changed, and a group of 12 special styles made up on special order according to designs furnished by college stores and student associations. The company had on hand, on 15 January 1993, an inventory which had been produced during 1992 at a cost of £250,000, but which, although still carried on the books of the company, was practically valueless. This inventory was equally divided between novelty items designed for the retail trade and cancelled orders of college co-operative stores and student associations.

Novelty items differed from standard lines in binding, size, shape, inside layout, and accessories such as locks, zipper closures, attached pencils, and the like. They were sold through jobbers along with the standard lines for the retail trade. Sales of the college lines were made during the summer for September and December delivery. Each order usually specified the number to be delivered in September and indicated the probable number wanted in December. The number to be delivered in December was subject to adjustment up or down, final determination of the exact amount being delayed until late November or early December, when college executives had a better indication of probable mid-year enrolment. In the past, such adjustments had been few and almost always had been increased above the original estimates. It had been the practice of the Barnstaple Company to make up each of these orders complete in time for the September delivery, stocking that portion of the order which was for future delivery. If an order was made up in two lots, the second lot was usually much smaller than the first and therefore the total unit cost of diaries made in the second lot was from five to seven per cent more than the total unit cost of diaries made in the first lot. College enrolments in 1992 proved somewhat smaller than anticipated, and as a result substantial portions of the college orders were cancelled. In fact, practically none of the special-order diaries which the Barnstaple Company had stocked for future delivery to college organizations in 1992 had been shipped. They represented a loss of approximately £125,000.

In round figures of sales and costs of the novelty and college lines as presented at the conference were as follows:

	College lines		Novelty lines	
Sales		£600,000		£650,000
Manufacturing cost of goods sold:				
Total labour cost	£187,500		£312,500[2]	
Total material used	187,500		187,500	
Factory overhead[3]	250,000		125,000	
Total manufacturing costs	625,000		625,000	
Inventory on hand at cost	125,000		125,000	
	£500,000	£500,000	£500,000	£500,000
Gross margin		£100,000		£150,000
Selling & administrative expense		125,000		150,000
Net profit or loss		**£(25,000)**		**£0**

Early in the conference it was pointed out that had the inventory carry-over from 1992 to 1993 been no greater than the usual nominal amount (in 1991 it had been less than £15,000) a satisfactory profit would have resulted. This statement induced a discussion of the college and novelty lines but little progress was made in working out a solution. After three hours, all that had been accomplished was clarification of the positions of the various executives.

The accountant maintained that both the college and novelty lines should be dropped on the basis that they were the cause of all the trouble. He said that there was no advantage in obtaining volume of output unless profit resulted therefrom. He urged that the activities of the company be somewhat curtailed. The sales manager agreed that the college lines should be discontinued, but urged that the novelty lines be retained. He pointed out that the college lines had been substantially responsible for the 1992 loss, that the gross margin on those lines was relatively small, and that they in no way contributed to the sale of the company's standard lines. The production manager objected to the retention of the novelty lines. He pointed out that while the gross margin on those lines was high, the selling expense was likewise high. He also made the statement that before 1989 the company had made few novelty items and had experienced no difficulty in selling its standard lines. He maintained that it was no fault of the production department that the company took a loss on the college lines during 1992.

At a second conference two days later, no further progress was made and the new general manager came to the conclusion that he would have to decide what should be done.

[1] These diaries often had the certificate of membership in the association printed in them. The certificate was filled out and the diary was given to the member without extra charge upon payment of the membership fee.

[2] Novelty items were made in small lots and therefore entailed a relatively high hand labour cost.

[3] Factory overhead consisted of such items of cost as heat, light, power, maintenance, supervision, depreciation, rent and supplies. Some of these costs varied with the rate of production; others remained relatively fixed on an annual basis irrespective of the volume of output. The college lines were produced in relatively large volume which made possible utilization of the company's machines and equipment. They were, therefore, assigned a larger share of the overhead than were the novelty lines.

Chapter 2

Problem solving and decision making

Introduction

The objective of this chapter is to set the scene and discuss the process and techniques involved in strategic marketing planning (SMP). As explained in the Preface, the overall objective of the book is to provide an opportunity to test your knowledge and understanding of the principles covered in marketing management texts and courses.

A secondary objective is to provide a linked set of exercises which, taken together, provide a comprehensive framework for the analysis and solution of a marketing problem. Such marketing problems may be academic, as is the situation when 'solving' case studies, or 'real world' (practitioner), when one has to address a particular aspect of marketing analysis and/or planning right up to the preparation of a complete marketing plan. In other words, the purpose is to develop analytic and planning *skills* of the kind called for in effective marketing practice.

In the preceding paragraph we distinguished between 'academic' and 'practitioner' needs. In reality they are much the same, with the only real difference being that the former addresses theoretical problems and the latter 'real-world' ones. Given the nature of real-world problems, especially those addressed by the members of professions such as architecture, engineering, law, medicine and marketing, the negative consequences of poor analysis, planning and implementation/action can be anything from serious to catastrophic. It is for this reason that would-be professionals who have mastered the knowledge base of their discipline are required to serve an apprenticeship under the supervision of a qualified practitioner before acquiring a 'licence' to practise.

In business, decisions are rarely so life-threatening as structures collapsing, equipment and machinery failing unexpectedly, or a doctor misdiagnosing a case of meningitis as a cold. To guard against such disasters the practical 'formation' of engineers, doctors, etc. has been more rigorous than that of business practitioners. However, all this may be changing. There is little or no call for unqualified accountants and the Chartered Institute of Marketing (CIM) is actively pursuing individual chartered status for its members who are qualified by examination, experience and continuing professional development for such status. At first such status, chartered marketer, may not be considered necessary for practice but, in the fullness of time, as chartered members demonstrate their greater professionalism it is to be anticipated that, like chartered accountants, such status will be considered a prerequisite for professional practice.

Meanwhile those responsible for the education and training of managers have been giving increased attention to the need for skills development in order to meet the express needs of employers. In the case of marketing, and its professional body the CIM, this need is recognized in the nature of the final examination for the award of its postgraduate Diploma in Marketing, which is a case study. Thus, the aim of the Analysis and Decision paper is set out as follows:

> The aim of this paper is to extend the practice of candidates in the qualitative and quantitative analysis of marketing situations, both to develop their powers of diagnosis and as a contribution to the creation of firm bases for decision making. Candidates should be able to:
>
> 1 Identify, define and rank the problem(s) contained in marketing case studies.
> 2 Formulate working hypotheses regarding the solution(s) to problems identified in marketing case studies.
> 3 Assemble, order, analyse and interpret both qualitative and quantitative data relating to a marketing case, using appropriate analytical procedures and models.
> 4 Describe and substantiate all working assumptions made regarding the case problem(s)' working hypotheses and data.
> 5 Generate and evaluate the expected outcomes of alternative solutions to case problem(s).
> 6 Formulate recommendations for action and feedback on case problem(s).
> 7 Prepare and present appropriate marketing case reports.

Clearly, the intention of this examination is to rehearse candidates in seven activities which are central to the practice of management as a basis for fulfilling these tasks in a real as opposed to vicarious setting.

Now the objective of the case method as pioneered by the Harvard Business School is to provide would-be managers with the opportunity to address real-world problems in a classroom setting. The advantages are obvious. In the real world a problem may require weeks or even months for its solution; in the classroom a matter of hours. Cases can be selected to exemplify specific issues whereas real-world problems occur and are often quite similar to previously experienced problems. As a result, in the real world practitioners may only be exposed to a narrow range of problems and so be uncertain how to react to those which fall outside the range of that experience. Ten years' 'experience' may well amount to the same year's experience repeated ten times over! Case study analysis allows the student to address a wide spectrum of problems and to develop skills in oral and written presentation so essential to persuading others to accept and implement a given course of action.

All seven activities looked for in the case study analysis are covered in this book, which follows quite closely the structure of leading textbooks dealing with strategic analysis and planning in a marketing context. Thus the book provides the framework for the analysis of business problems and the development of workable solutions. Individual exercises may be used to address specific aspects of this activity while the complete set can be used to help solve a case study or a real-world problem – the process is the same. While the practitioner will apply this process and appropriate techniques to the problem confronting him or her, the student will wish to use such techniques on a case study. To illustrate how to apply the various techniques, analytical frameworks and procedures described in the text refer to the short case study appended to Chapter 1 which will be referred to where relevant.

Before working through the exercises, however, it will be useful to examine five topics which are common to them all and provide the background for the book as a whole:

1 The concept of corporate strategy and the normative decision-making process.
2 Problem definition.
3 Decision making under uncertainty
   ● the quantity and quality of information
   ● degrees of certainty
   ● hard and soft data
   ● decision trees and Bayesian analysis.
4 Data collection
   ● closing the information gap
   ● qualitative and quantitative data
   ● expected value of perfect information (EVPI)
   ● analysis.
5 Diagnostics
   ● scaling and rating tables
   ● matrix analysis.

The concept of corporate strategy and the normative decision-making process

In his book *Strategy and Structure*, Alfred D. Chandler (1962) defines corporate strategy as:

> The determination of the basic long-term goals and objectives of an enterprise, and the adoption of courses of action and the allocation of resources necessary for carrying out these goals.

This definition suggests three distinct phases in the strategic process:

- appreciation;
- plan;
- implementation.

In turn, these three phases lead to the four fundamental questions which face the problem solver/decision maker which we introduced in the previous chapter:

- Where am I now?
- Where do I want to go?
- How do I get there?
- How will I know when I've arrived?

As we observed, each of these questions may be further subdivided and it is a matter for the individual to decide how much detail is necessary in order to take an informed decision. For example Kotler (1988) proposes:

- Diagnosis: where is the company now, and why?
- Prognosis: where is the company headed?
- Objectives: where should the company be headed?
- Strategy: what is the best way to get there?
- Tactics: what specific actions should be taken, by whom, and when?
- Control: what measures should be watched to indicate whether the company is succeeding?

Similarly, the Marketing Science Institute (Robinson and Luck, 1964) developed a model called APACS (Adaptive Planning and Control Sequence) which contains eight steps:

- Step 1   Define problem and set objectives.
- Step 2   Appraise overall situation.
- Step 3   Determine the tasks to be accomplished and identify the means to achieving these aims.

- Step 4 Identify alternative plans and mixes.
- Step 5 Estimate the expected results arising from implementation of the alternative plans.
- Step 6 Managerial review and decision.
- Step 7 Feedback of results and post-audit.
- Step 8 Adapt programme if required.

Clearly, there is a considerable overlap between these two prescriptions and countless others like them. Our own structure, introduced in the previous chapter, combines elements of both. If you wish to insert or delete steps in the process, then there is no reason not to if the circumstances suggest you should.

(In passing, you may have noticed that there is an implicit assumption made here that corporate strategy and marketing strategy are the same. In our view, for all practical purposes they are! This view is based on the belief that business strategy must be shaped by market forces and so is a 'marketing' strategy. Further, with the exception of large, multidivisional companies operating in distinct markets which need an overarching 'corporate' strategy to co-ordinate and integrate the separate 'marketing' strategies of its various SBUs, the marketing strategy is synonymous with the corporate strategy.)

Problem definition

Green and Tull (1978) point out that decisions are made to solve problems. A problem may be said to exist when the following conditions are faced:

1 There are one or more objectives to be met.
2 There are two or more alternative courses of action that could be taken.
3 There is uncertainty as to which course of action will maximize the attainment of the objective.

Implicit in these three conditions are two others:

4 The problem exists in an environment that affects the objectives, the possible courses of action, and the degree of uncertainty concerning the outcome of each.
5 There are one or more decision makers.

While marketing problems share common elements with other kinds of problem they also possess some characteristics which call for particular care. Among these characteristics may be numbered:

1 Many marketing problems are multidimensional and very complex and so cannot be expected to yield direct one-to-one relationships of the kind found in the experimental sciences.

2 Many marketing problems are more or less unique in the sense that they call for a decision on a combination of factors and circumstances that are unlikely to be encountered again in precisely the same form.
3 A large proportion of marketing problems concern future decisions and so contain greater uncertainty than those concerned with present decisions, e.g. with production or distribution.

A further issue associated with the identification and solution of marketing problems is that because they are concerned with the interaction of buyers and sellers in negotiating exchange transactions they possess a dynamism which is absent from many other problems.

Because of these characteristics, problem definition is often fraught with difficulty in a marketing context but it remains true that clear definition of the problem is a major factor in developing an effective solution. It follows that special care must be given to this phase of strategic planning. Huber (1980) identified three tendencies which frequently interfere with adequate problem specification and definition:

1 The tendency to define the problem in terms of the proposed solution.
2 The tendency to focus on narrow, lower order goals.
3 The tendency to diagnose the problem in terms of its symptoms.

The first tendency is a widespread and pervasive phenomenon which has sometimes been characterized as 'a solution searching for a problem'. The more 'expert' a person is the greater the likelihood that he or she will fall victim of this fallacy and tend to recast or interpret facts in terms of his or her own selective expectations and perception. Thus, all problems become seen as manifestations of the problem solver's own expertise and it is no accident that as top managers emerge from given disciplines and functions they tend to view all the problems they encounter from that perspective and classify them as 'finance', 'marketing' or 'production' problems. The real danger of this tendency is that it excludes the consideration of alternative explanations.

The second tendency is also commonplace among managers who seek to reduce problems to a comfortable order of magnitude which falls well within their existing experience and competence. Such managers will be happy with fine-tuning the marketing mix, but will shy away from a radical programme of innovation and new product development which will lead them into new and unfamiliar markets.

The third tendency, of diagnosing problems in terms of their symptoms, is also familiar but much less dangerous than the two previous diversions from the search for alternatives. Indeed, in many circumstances good diagnosis must be a sequential process in which you relate the symptoms to the most likely cause and prescribe accordingly. Most headaches are temporary, and acute phenomena may arise from a large number of causes which are equally temporary and acute. The need is to alleviate the symptoms and monitor their progression. If after twenty-four hours all is well and the symptoms do not return, we will discount the cause as unimportant. But, if the symptoms persist, we will probe more deeply and try other remedies until, by a process of trial and error, we discover the true cause. Such a procedure exemplifies well the concept of the expected value of information for, in the absence of highly distinctive and unmistakable symptoms, one does not admit everyone who complains of a headache to hospital for a brain scan!

The process of trial and error suggested above is reflected in Figure 2.1, which sees problem recognition leading to a preliminary specification firmed up into a more precise definition following exploratory investigation. This definition is tested by reference to other available information (secondary data) with either a solution being found or research commissioned to secure missing data.

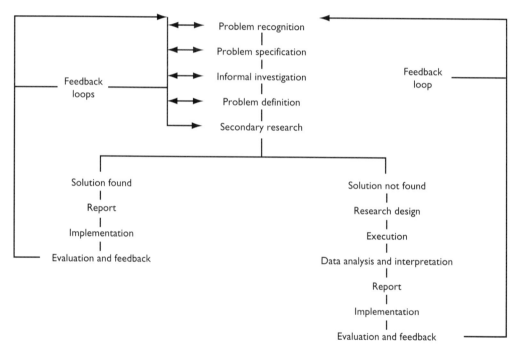

Figure 2.1 The market research process

Defining and solving problems usually involves making decisions under varying degrees of uncertainty. We look briefly at these issues in the next section.

Decision making under uncertainty

Problems exist because we lack perfect information. It follows that establishing what information is needed to solve a problem and then acquiring it are critical skills of the analyst/planner. This task is not without difficulties. First, data are frequently incomplete; second, much data is presented in the form of opinion; third, data may only be inferred from the apparent relationship between facts or events. In consequence of these difficulties all data must be screened for their accuracy, validity and reliability as a preliminary to deciding whether the information may be used to help solve the problem. Issues of accuracy, reliability and validity are treated at length in many textbooks so only a brief review will be given here.

While complete accuracy is *truth* it would be wrong to infer that less than complete accuracy is untruth and therefore unacceptable. In a business context it is rare that we require the degree of precision necessary in the scientific laboratory or even the engineering workshop. A reasonable estimate will often suffice. What is reasonable depends upon the circumstances and may vary by several percentage points around the true value; for example an estimate of market size. Essentially, the need for accuracy depends upon how sensitive the final outcome of the analysis is to changes in the value of constituent elements – if the end result appears to be largely insensitive, then approximation will suffice; if highly sensitive, then the more accurate the estimate the better.

The concepts of *reliability* and *validity* are frequent sources of confusion but a clear definition and explanation is offered by Martin and Bateson (1986) as follows:

I **Reliability** concerns the extent to which measurement is repeatable and consistent; that is, free from random errors. An unbiased measurement consists of two parts: a systematic component, representing the true value of the variable, and a random component due to imperfections in the measurement process. The smaller the error component, the more reliable the measurement.

   Reliable measures, sometimes referred to as good measures, are those which measure a variable precisely and consistently. At least four related factors determine how 'good' a measure is:

   (a) *Precision:* How free are measurements from random errors? This is denoted by the number of 'significant figures' in the measurement. Note that accuracy and precision are not synonymous: accuracy concerns systematic error (bias) and can therefore be regarded as an aspect of validity (see below). A clock may tell the time with great precision (to within a millisecond), yet be inaccurate because it is set to the wrong time.

   (b) *Sensitivity:* Do small changes in the true value invariably lead to changes in the measured value?

(c) **Resolution:** What is the smallest change in the true value that can be detected?

(d) **Consistency:** Do repeated measures of the same thing produce the same results?

2 **Validity** concerns the extent to which a measurement actually measures those features the investigator wishes to measure, and provides information that is relevant to the questions being asked. Validity refers to the relation between a variable (such as a measure of behaviour) and what it is supposed to measure or predict about the world.

   Valid measures, sometimes referred to as **right** measures, are those which actually answer the questions being asked. To decide whether a measure is valid ('right'), at least two separate points must be considered:

(a) **Accuracy:** Is the measurement process unbiased, such that measured values correspond with the true values? Measurements are accurate if they are relatively free from systematic errors (whereas precise measurements are relatively free from random errors).

(b) **Specificity:** To what extent does the measure describe what it is supposed to describe, and nothing else?

Given that some factors are more important than others (we look specifically at critical success factors in Chapter 4) an ability to isolate these is vital, as we will then be able to concentrate our limited resources on them. When using data from published sources we must distinguish between the credibility to be attached to government statistics gathered by census and estimates extrapolated from samples by trade associations, consultants and those with vested interests in the interpretation of the data they convey. We must also be conscious of recency and assess how a delay in publishing data may affect its validity. We must also be sensitive to changes in the collection and recording of data over time and be satisfied as to the comparability of such data.

In the above discussion of the nature of information reference was made to the degree of certainty that may be attached to data and data sources. Some further clarification may be helpful.

Faced with the need to make a decision there are three possible states of mind:

1 **Certainty** – the decision maker has perfect information and *knows* the outcome of a given combination of events with the result that they may be predicted precisely, e.g. an eclipse of the sun, high water at Tower Bridge in a month's time, the behaviour of falling objects, etc.

2 **Risk** – the decision maker has extensive past experience or knowledge of similar events to the extent that he or she can predict the general outcome but not the specific result of any given event. For example O-level passes used to be based on the expectation that students in the top forty per cent of the ability range would be able to pass them. It follows that if I predict that any given child will fail, I have a sixty per cent chance of being right. It also follows that if I acquire additional information, such as previous school reports, I can improve the accuracy of my prediction in any particular case and so reduce the risk of being wrong.

3 **Uncertainty** – as with risk there are several possible outcomes, but in this case one has little or no prior experience or knowledge and so cannot assign an *objective* probability to the possible outcomes.

The inability to assign an objective probability does not prevent us from developing subjective expectations about the likelihood of a given event and acting upon our *judgement*. Indeed, the great majority of decisions we make are a combination of facts and judgement and, in a business context, preferment and promotion are given to those who demonstrate good judgement, by which we mean that their decisions are more often right than wrong. In essence, the key to successful decision making would seem to lie in the ability to specify the alternatives, the likelihood of their occurrence and the consequences associated with each.

In the case of important decisions where the consequences or outcomes may have a major impact, we must be prepared to invest more time and effort into data gathering and analysis before exercising judgement. To assist managers to improve their decision-making ability when combining facts and judgement, theorists have developed the concept of *decision trees* and related this to *Bayes' theorem* as a means of combining prior estimates with new information to generate a set of revised or posterior probabilities. Only a brief reprise can be offered here but a full discussion of the issues is to be found in the references cited at the end of the book.

As Hatton *et al.* (op. cit.) explain:

> A decision tree is a conceptual map which catalogues possible decisions and the outcomes. It is particularly useful if you are required to make a number of decisions, each affected by previous decisions.
>
> The technique allows the knock-on impact of decisions to be considered. Used in conjunction with assessments of *probability* it is possible to make very sophisticated judgements that are supported by quantitative evaluation.

An example of a decision tree is illustrated in Figure 2.2.

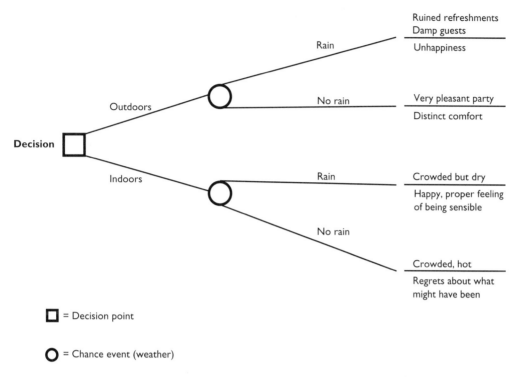

Figure 2.2 Decision tree (*Source*: Magee, J.F. (1964). Decision trees for decision making, *Harvard Business Review*, July–August)

In simple terms, probability reflects the likelihood of an event expressed on a scale which runs from 1.0, which is equivalent to certainty, to 0.0, which is equivalent to impossible. In managerial decision making three kinds of probability may be involved – *a priori, relative frequency* and *subjective*.

An *a priori* probability expresses the frequency with which an event may occur in terms of the total number of possible outcomes, so that the *a priori* probability of obtaining a head in coin tossing is 0.5, of a six when throwing a dice 0.166, of the ace of spades on a single draw from a pack of cards 0.019, and so on. This is a concept of probability with which we are all familiar but it is one which has little application save in games of chance or for certain kinds of statistical analysis.

The *relative frequency* method of assigning probabilities is much more useful in managerial decision making and is the technique used for assigning risk in the sense in which we defined it earlier. As the term suggests, probabilities of this kind are based upon knowledge concerning the frequency with which an event has occurred in the past, thus enabling us to express a view as to its likelihood of re-occurrence in the future. This concept is central to the whole theory of sampling as used in market research.

However, the use of relative frequencies depends upon the availability of objective information concerning the previous occurrence of events identical to the one which we are trying to predict. But, as we argued earlier when defining uncertainty and the nature of marketing problems, the dynamic and interactive nature of most marketing activities militates against identical occurrences and it is this which makes prediction of marketing events so difficult. For this reason we have to depend upon the experience, skill and judgement of the decision maker and use his or her *subjective* expectation of the occurrence of an event as the basis for an actual decision. Bayes' theorem provides an analytical framework for combining these subjective expectations with the decision tree to enable us to select which of the available alternatives offers the best solution. (A discussion of the selection of a decision criterion and a simple worked example of a decision tree for launching a new product are to be found in *Marketing Strategy and Management*, pp. 307–311.)

Data collection

While Bayesian analysis offers a structured approach to combining objective and subjective information, like any other analytical technique it is completely dependent upon the quality of the data used. (Remember GIGO – Garbage In Garbage Out). A key aspect of decision making is deciding what information will improve the diagnosis of a problem, and how to acquire and assess the value of such information. In this section we address these issues.

Earlier, when introducing the topic of 'Decision making under uncertainty' we made the point that problems exist because we lack perfect information. Given that strategic planning is concerned with the future, which by definition is uncertain, it is clear that we can never hope to have perfect information about it. Inevitably there will be a 'gap' between what we know and what we would like to know. To close this gap we need to gather additional data. Hatton *et al.* (op. cit.) recommend that we handle the information gap as follows:

- Identify clearly what information you want and have not got. Are you sure you need it? Remember to make the distinction between need to know and nice to know information.
- Assess the cost/benefit of collecting this information.
- Remember that marketing research (MR) is an investment in the information resource and should be approached with the same care as any other investment decision.
- Consider the process for providing the missing information to the organization and be able to make clear recommendations for filling the information gap.

In recognizing that data gathering incurs costs and that these need to be traded off against the benefits received, decision analysts have developed a useful technique based upon the Bayesian methodology introduced earlier. First, however, it will be useful to establish some guidelines for assessing the value of information. A useful checklist contained in *Research for Marketing* (Baker, 1991) is reproduced in Table 2.1.

Table 2.1 Factors determining the value of information

Factors indicating high information value

1 The cost of selecting a 'bad' alternative (go error) or failing to select the best alternative (no-go error) would be relatively high.
2 There is a very high degree of uncertainty about which alternative to choose, based on existing information.
3 Survey research information is likely to reduce a substantial portion of the uncertainty.
4 There is a high likelihood that survey research will be effective at reducing the uncertainty.

Factors indicating low information value

1 The cost of making either a go or no-go error would be relatively small.
2 There is relatively little uncertainty about the decision, based only on existing information.
3 Survey research information will remove only a small portion of the uncertainty about the decision.
4 There is no way to be sure that survey research information will be effective at reducing uncertainty.

Source: Alreck, P. and Settle, R.B. (1985). *The Survey Research Handbook*. Homewood, Illinois: Irwin.

Bearing in mind Hatton *et al.*'s advice that we must distinguish between need to know and nice to know, the value of additional information must be judged against our level of existing and prior knowledge. Thus the value of additional information is relative to the improvement in overall knowledge and the reduction in perceived uncertainty which this offers. To calculate the expected value of information (EVI) we must first construct a decision pay-off table of the kind illustrated in Table 2.2.

This pay-off table summarizes the alternatives facing a food company which is considering substituting a cheaper ingredient in one of its products. Such a change would save £2 million; however, if customers can detect this change they are likely to switch to other brands, which could cost up to £14 million. If twenty per cent of the customers notice the change, then the outcomes are as summarized in Table 2.2, the key figure in which is the EMV. This indicates that if twenty per cent switch, there will be a loss of £2.8 million (£14 million × 0.2)

Table 2.2 Decision pay-off table

Actual outcome	Estimated probability (%)	Change ingredient (£)	Do not change ingredient (£)
Customer can detect the difference	20	−14m	0m
Customer cannot detect the difference	80	2m	0m
Expected monetary value (EMV)		−1.2m	0m

against which there will be a saving of £1.6 million (£2 million × 0.8) so that the EMV is £1.2 million. Clearly, the critical issue is how many customers will notice the change and how much would I be prepared to pay to get this information? The answer, in theory, is up to £1.6 million, which is the maximum gain if eighty per cent of the customers cannot detect the difference. Common sense tells us that if this resulted in twenty per cent switching to a competitor we stand to lose £1.2 million so we shouldn't do this, but if only ten per cent switched then the EMV would be £400,000. Only you can decide how much you would spend to get clear feedback by testing customer reactions before making the change. In all probability, conducting tests to establish likely switching behaviour would cost less than £50,000, which seems a reasonable investment in relation to the possible gains or losses that might accrue without this information.

Analysis of data

The analysis of data is a major subject in its own right. It calls for both technical knowledge and skills and a primary objective of this book is to provide the user with an opportunity to test and apply these. It follows that this short section can only serve to remind the reader of where to look for advice.

So far we have dealt with issues of *problem definition, decision making under uncertainty* and *data collection* in order to emphasize the importance of a structured approach to the solving of business problems. We have also discussed the concept of the expected value of perfect information to assist the decision maker in deciding how much time, effort and money can be invested in gathering data as the basis for making an informed decision. However, in this task we are faced with three major difficulties – data are frequently incomplete, much information is presented in the form of opinion, or may only be inferred from the apparent relationship between facts or events. It follows that a major task of the analyst is to screen all the available data or evidence for accuracy, validity and reliability as a preliminary to determining whether any relationships exist between acceptable facts that are suggestive of a solution to the problem in hand.

The mark of a good analyst is the ability to isolate the critical factors and then obtain the most accurate data available concerning them. As noted earlier, when using published sources the analyst must distinguish between the credibility attached to data collected by census and that collected by survey and, even more so, that obtained by self-reporting procedures. The analyst must also be conscious of recency and assess how the delay in publishing data may affect its current validity. The analyst must also be sensitive to changes in the collection and recording of data over time and be satisfied as to the comparability of such data.

Such strictures are all very well when dealing with data from published sources. How do analysts deal with opinion and hearsay? Much information in business reports falls into this category and is often conflicting in its indication of the true state of affairs. A classic example is to be found in the Barnstaple Company case study, which is used in this book as a basis for demonstrating the application of the various analytical approaches and techniques used. In this case study the three executive managers responsible for the finance, production and sales functions each attribute the company's problems to a different cause! However, by carefully adducing factual data in the case, or inferences which may be drawn from these data with a very high degree of confidence, it can be clearly demonstrated that only one manager's opinion is acceptable. Herein lies the skill of the analyst – an ability to pick out relevant pieces of information while discarding those which serve only to confuse the issue and so identify the real functional relationships.

It is possible to distinguish three different levels of analysis in this sorting and synthesizing process – deduction, inference and the formulation of assumptions. A deduction is made when the analyst derives a logically necessary conclusion about a specific case from perfect information concerning the general case. For example all retailers of cars operate on a fifteen per cent gross margin; the XYZ Company is a retailer of cars; *deduction* – the XYZ Company operates on a fifteen per cent gross margin.

The status of an *inference* is less clear-cut. An inference may be defined as the interpretation placed upon evidence by an observer. From this it follows that this may be anything from excellent – there is a very high probability that it is an accurate interpretation – to very poor – it is not an accurate interpretation of reality. Assuming, however, that the correct inference is drawn, then the distinction between an inference and a deduction is that there is always an element of uncertainty associated with an inference while there is none in the case of a correct deduction. However, by linking logical deductions with reasonable inferences the analyst can go a long way towards the solution of a problem.

The need for assumptions only arises where there is an absence of evidence necessary to link other evidence which appears to bear upon the problem – a frequent occurrence in business decision making! Assumptions may be of two kinds – working assumptions and critical assumptions. Working assumptions are those necessary to move an argument along and provide links in the chain of reasoning. Unlike critical assumptions, they are not vital to the final decision. Assumptions should only be made as a last resort where other information is not available. When setting out an assumption, and especially a critical assumption, it is important to state clearly the evidence used, the reasons for selecting or rejecting particular points, and the precise form of the final assumption made. Only by careful attention to these factors will the analyst be able to communicate the thought processes leading to the conclusion. Without such explanation the argument will be open to criticism and lack conviction. We return to the formulation of assumptions in Chapter 6.

Diagnostics

Scaling and rating tables

The discussion of data collection and analysis makes it clear that problem solving requires the decision maker to handle a combination of objective facts together with a wide range of attitudes, opinions and conjecture. The latter, subjective, data are often the most important when addressing marketing problems. While such data are usually expressed in verbal statements – 'I prefer Pepsi to Coke' – their use in diagnosis and analysis will be greatly increased if we can convert them into numerical statements which can then be compared and diagnosed using quantitative techniques.

This need for quantitative measurement is particularly strong when dealing with attitudinal data, for the basic reason that attitude has a directional quality. It connotes a preference regarding the outcomes involving the object, evaluation of the object, or positive–neutral–negative affectations for the object. To capture these attributes the assignment of a numerical value by means of *scaling* is a widely used practice in marketing research and analysis.

There are four types of scale – *nominal, ordinal, interval* and *ratio* – each of which possesses different properties.

1 **Nominal scales** are the weakest form of scale, in which the number assigned serves only to identify the objects under consideration. Library classification schemes employ nominal scales, as does the Standard Industrial Classification (SIC), such that members of the same class will be assigned the same number but each class will have a different number. By extending the number it is possible to achieve finer and finer distinctions until a unique number is assigned to a specific object, e.g. a telephone number.

2 **Ordinal scales** seek to impose more structure on objects by rank ordering them in terms of some property such as height or weight. As with nominal scales, identical objects are given the same number but the ordinal scale has the added property that it can tell us something about the *direction* or relative standing of one object to another, e.g. I may represent the smallest member of a group such

that we can safely say that 2 is bigger than 1, 5 is bigger than 2 and 17 is bigger than 5. However, this is all we can say (other than reversing the scale) and in order to be able to draw conclusions about differences between the numbers we must know something about the interval between the numbers.

3 **Interval scales** have this property in that they are founded on the assumption of equal intervals between numbers, i.e. the space between 5 and 10 is the same as the space between 45 and 50 and, in both cases, this distance is five times as great as that between 1 and 2 or 11 and 12, etc. However, it must be stressed that while we may compare the magnitude of the differences between numbers we cannot make statements about them unless the scale possesses an absolute zero, in which case we would have a ratio scale.

4 **Ratio scales** are the most powerful and possess all the properties of nominal, ordinal and interval scales, while in addition they permit absolute comparisons of the objects, e.g. 6 feet is twice as high as 3 feet and six times as high as 1 foot.

Among the more important scales used in marketing are:

- Thurstone scales.
- Likert scales.
- Guttmann scales.
- The semantic differential technique.

Thurstone scales were first introduced by L. L. Thurstone in 1928 and have been very widely used ever since. In essence, a Thurstone scale is an attempt to construct an interval scale by selecting a set of statements about a subject which range from very favourable to very unfavourable expressions of attitude towards the subject, with each statement appearing to be equidistant from those on either side of it. Scales may contain eleven, nine or seven statements, which are chosen by a panel of judges from a pool so as to achieve the property of equal-appearing intervals, and respondents are asked to select the statement which most accurately reflects their attitude. A score is assigned to each statement and is used, often in conjunction with scores for other sets of statements, in order to provide a summary statement of attitude towards the object of inquiry.

Likert scales differ from Thurstone scales in that respondents are presented with a series of statements and asked to indicate their degree of agreement/ disagreement with each. Respondents are usually offered five categories – Strongly Agree, Agree, Uncertain, Disagree, Strongly Disagree, though three to seven divisions are used by some researchers – and are asked to select the position corresponding most closely with their opinion. By scoring a series of statements on a given subject, e.g. qualities of a brand, content of an advertisement, it is possible to construct a generalized attitude towards the object with an indication of the *intensity* with which the attitude is held.

Guttmann scaling represents an attempt to ensure a highly desirable property of an attitude scale which is only partially achieved by the Thurstone and

Likert methods – the property of unidimensionality, i.e. all the statements used belong to the same dimension. The construction of Guttmann scales is more complex and laborious than for Thurstone and Likert scales and is described at some length by Moser and Kalton (1971) – as are all the other methods referred to here. However, relatively little use is made of the method in marketing research.

In contrast, the *semantic differential technique* developed by Osgood *et al.* (1952) is very widely used, largely because it is much simpler to construct than any of the scales discussed so far and yet yields a very high measure of agreement with these more elaborate measures. The method consists of a series of bipolar adjectives (strong–weak, good–bad, etc.) separated usually by between five and nine points. Respondents are asked to tick the point which best indicates their attitude. Scale positions are sometimes qualified, for example:

Extremely good
Very good
Fairly good
Neither good nor bad
Fairly bad
Very bad
Extremely bad.

However, such qualification tends to discourage selection of the extreme positions.

By assigning values to the verbal statements used in rating scales or by asking respondents to indicate their strength of feeling by assigning a numerical value to it, it is possible to create powerful diagnostic tools. We make extensive use of such rating scales in this book. The value of such scales is enhanced when dealing with objects or concepts which possess several different dimensions if we combine them into a *factor rating* table.

For example suppose we are making a competitor analysis of the five leading suppliers of earth-moving equipment in terms of the five attributes (or factors) which research has shown to be important in buying decisions – price, performance (cubic capacity of shovel), reliability, availability of service, and delivery. While all these factors are important in coming to a decision some are clearly more important than others and this can be reflected in our analysis by assigning different *weights* to them. Similarly, we can score each supplier in terms of how well they perform on each of the five key attributes – possibly using data collected from buyers using rating scales. By combining these data in a rating table we can quickly establish the relative standing of the five suppliers, as shown in Table 2.3.

From this table it is clear that Firm E emerges as the preferred supplier, despite having the highest price and the poorest delivery, due to the higher weighting given to performance, reliability and service as choice factors. It is

Table 2.3 A factor rating table

Factor	Weighting	Firm A	Firm B	Firm C	Firm D	Firm E
Price	6	8	5	7	7	4
Performance	8	7	8	6	7	9
Reliability	10	7	8	7	6	9
Service	9	7	9	8	6	9
Delivery	5	8	7	7	8	6
Score		277	290	267	252	297
Ranking		**3**	**2**	**4**	**5**	**1**

also clear that there is a considerable gap between Firms B and E and Firms A, C and D in their overall evaluation. Factor rating tables such as this offer considerable benefits in enabling the decision maker to capture and structure complex data and, through the assignment of weightings which reflect their own preferences, distinguish between what otherwise might appear to be closely matched alternatives.

Similar benefits are also to be found in the use of simple matrices using two dimensions with two or three alternatives associated with each dimension. Igor Ansoff's growth/vector matrix, the Boston box, Shell's directional policy matrix and perceptual mapping are well-known examples of such diagnostic frameworks which you will have already encountered in your studies. We make extensive use of these in this book and fuller explanations will be given when they are introduced.

Summary

In this chapter we have looked at five topics which are common to the analysis of marketing (and other business) problems:

- Normative decision making
- Problem definition
- Decision making under uncertainty
- Data collection
- Diagnostics.

All of these subjects will occur throughout the series of exercises contained in the book and the reader should refer back to this chapter as required if further clarification is needed.

Chapter 3

Developing a marketing orientation

Introduction

As a practitioner or a student taking a formal course in marketing you will know that marketing is both simple and complex. As stated elsewhere (Baker, 1996), the problem is that most people believe that they know what marketing is when they don't. One reason for this is that we are all involved in marketing and: 'The enigma of marketing is that it is one of man's oldest activities and yet it is regarded as the most recent of the business disciplines' (Baker, 1976).

Marketing came into existence with the first barter exchange when someone realized that exchanges add value for both parties. It was this recognition that led to the development of task specialization. This was the first real step forward in economic development. Like many other crafts or practices such as architecture, engineering, or medicine, marketing has evolved over the centuries to the point that it is now widely regarded as a profession with an established body of knowledge, the mastery of which is necessary for successful practice. Given that the primary purpose of this book is to test your knowledge and the ability to apply it in practice it would seem sensible to start by ensuring that you have a clear understanding of what marketing is.

In this chapter we start with a few definitions of marketing as a reminder of some of the many interpretations that have been placed upon it. Based on these definitions we will see that marketing may be classified as a *process*, a *concept* or a *philosophy of business*, and as an *orientation*. Two exercises are provided, the first to answer the question: 'What business are you in?', the second designed to diagnose just how marketing orientated you are.

Definitions

In *Marketing*, 6th edition (Baker, 1996) there are sixteen different definitions of marketing, largely organized in chronological order. These are:

1 The function of marketing is the establishment of contact (Cherington, 1920).
2 Marketing is the process of determining consumer demand for a product or service, motivating its sale and distributing it into ultimate consumption at a profit (Brech, 1953).
3 Marketing is not only much broader than selling, it is not a specialized activity at all. It encompasses the entire business. It is the whole business seen from the point of view of its final result, that is, from the customer's point of view. Concern and responsibility for marketing must therefore permeate all areas of the enterprise (Drucker, 1954).
4 Marketing is the distinguishing, the unique function of the business (Drucker, 1954).
5 Marketing is the performance of business activities that direct the flow of goods and services from producer to consumer or user.
   ● Marketing is the creation of time, place and possession utilities.
   ● Marketing moves goods from place to place, stores them, and effects changes in ownership by buying and selling them.
   ● Marketing consists of the activities of buying, selling, transporting and storing goods.
   ● Marketing includes those business activities involved in the flow of goods and services between producers and consumers (Converse, Huegy and Mitchell, 1965).
6 Marketing is the process whereby society, to supply its consumption needs, evolves distributive systems composed of participants, who, interacting under constraints – technical (economic) and ethical (social) – create the transactions or flows which resolve market separations and result in exchange and consumption (Bartels, 1968).
7 Marketing is the set of human activities directed at facilitating and consummating exchanges (Kotler, 1972).
8 Marketing is concerned with the creation and maintenance of mutually satisfying exchange relationships (Baker, 1976).
9 The purpose of a business is to create and keep a customer (Levitt, 1983).
10 Marketing is the business function that identifies current unfilled needs and wants, defines and measures their magnitude, determines which target markets the organization can best serve, and decides on appropriate products, services, and programmes to serve these markets. Thus, marketing serves as the link between a society's needs and its pattern of industrial response (Kotler, 1988).
11 Marketing is both a set of activities performed by organizations and a social process. In other words, marketing exists at both the micro and macro levels. Micro marketing is the performance of activities which seek to accomplish an organization's objectives by anticipating customer or client needs and directing a flow of need-satisfying goods and services from producer to customer or client.

Macro marketing is a social process which directs an economy's flow of goods and services from producers to customers in a way which effectively matches supply and demand and accomplishes the objectives of society (McCarthy and Perreault, 1994).

12 Marketing is the process of planning and executing the conception, pricing, promotion and distribution of ideas, goods and services to create exchanges that satisfy individual and organizational goals (American Marketing Association).

13 Marketing is the management process responsible for identifying, anticipating and satisfying consumers' requirements profitably (Chartered Institute of Marketing).

14 Activities that facilitate and expedite satisfying exchange relationships through the creation, distribution, promotion and pricing of products (goods, services and ideas) (Marketing Association of Australia and New Zealand, MAANZ).

15 Marketing is selling goods that don't come back to people who do.

16 The delivery of a standard of living.

Faced with an even longer list of definitions, Crosier (1975) proposed that they could be classified into three major groupings:

1 Definitions which conceive of marketing as a *process* 'enacted via the marketing channel connecting the producing company with its market', e.g. 'The primary management function which organises and directs the aggregate of business activities involved in converting customer purchasing power into effective demand for a specific product or service and in moving the product or service to the final customer or user, so as to achieve company-set profit or other objectives' (Rodger, 1971).

2 Definitions which see marketing as a *concept* or a *philosophy of business* – 'the idea that marketing is a social exchange process involving willing consumers and producers', e.g. 'Selling is preoccupied with the seller's need to convert his product into cash; marketing with the idea of satisfying the needs of the customer by means of the product and the whole cluster of things associated with creating, delivering and finally consuming it' (Levitt, 1960).

3 Definitions which emphasize marketing as an *orientation* – 'present to some degree in both consumers and producer: the phenomenon which makes the concept and the process possible'. Only one example is cited by Crosier (from the philosopher Erich Fromm) and is felt to be an unconvincing argument in favour of a third category beyond the view of marketing as a function or as a concept. In our view, *orientation* is implicit in the *philosophy of business* adopted by an organization.

As noted earlier, our own listing is essentially in chronological order and so reflects the change in emphasis as the discipline has evolved. At the beginning of this century the prevailing view was that marketing was all about putting sellers and potential buyers in touch with one another. This *functional* approach, which is concerned with the *process* by which exchanges are organized and implemented, still lies at the very heart of marketing.

However, by the middle of this century the historical imbalance of an excess of demand over supply had begun to swing, at least in the more advanced economies, towards a potential excess of supply over demand. As a result of this shift, the age-old preoccupation with the creation of supply was replaced with greater emphasis upon demand and its stimulation. This change of emphasis is reflected in the 1950s by the recognition of marketing as the *key* business discipline. With the accent now being on the consumer rather than the producer, marketing is seen as a *concept* or *philosophy* which, in turn, requires organizations wishing to put this philosophy into practice to adopt a marketing *orientation*.

Marketing as a philosophy of business

One of the most influential and widely read contributions to the literature of marketing is Ted Levitt's 'Marketing myopia' (*Harvard Business Review*, 1960). It was this article that crystallized the distinction between marketing as a business function or process and marketing as an all-embracing philosophy for the direction and conduct of exchange relationships.

The essence of Levitt's argument is deceptively simple. Human beings have a fairly limited set of basic needs. Human progress and standard of living is based upon finding new and better ways of satisfying these needs and substituting these for old ways and methods. Individuals and organizations see innovation (the creation of new solutions) as the way to change the old order of things and increase their own competitiveness. But, while some individuals and organizations promote change others, through inertia or complacency, or both, resist change. As a result, they are doomed to inevitable failure.

As Levitt points out, the paradox is that 'every declining industry was once a growth industry'. In other words, the birth of an industry or the development of a new market is invariably based on innovation – a new and better way of serving old needs. The paradox is that as innovators succeed they lose sight of the source of their success. Instead of seeking even better ways of serving their customers they perceive this as making their existing skills and resources obsolete and so focus on incremental improvement of their existing technology and procedures. In other words, they become introspective and self-serving rather than outward-looking and concerned with satisfying their customers' needs better.

Levitt crystallizes his arguments by contending that the organization should define itself and its mission in terms of the needs that it serves and the benefits that it offers rather than the nature of its technology and the attributes of the products or services it offers for sale. If you run a railway you should consider yourself as in the 'transportation' business. If you make movies you are in the 'entertainment' business, and if you drill for oil you are in the 'energy' business.

Such a definition is important in defining the generic need but this concept needs to be refined into an understanding of consumer wants before it can be used operationally.

A *need* is something fundamental to the maintenance of life, such as food, drink, shelter and clothing. Needs are largely physiological in the sense that they are basic and instinctive drives with which we are born. It is clear, however, that a need may be satisfied by any one of a large number of alternatives: for example thirst may be satisfied by water, tea, coffee, beer, wine, and so forth. The availability of alternative means of satisfying a need constitutes *choice*, provision of which is central to the practice of marketing. In the absence of substitute, or alternative, goods there can be no choice, and needs and wants become synonymous.

Where there is more than one way of satisfying a basic need, physiological drives will be modified by economic, sociological and psychological factors. Variations in these factors will predispose individuals to prefer a specific alternative and this preference constitutes a *want*.

Definition of the need served and alternative approaches to achieving this – the provision of choice to meet wants – is the first step in developing an effective marketing strategy. Exercise 3.1 invites you to define the business you are in. If you are a practitioner, then you should use your own organization; if a student seeking to solve a particular case study, you should use this as the basis for your answer but, otherwise, use the Barnstaple Company case study, which is the Appendix to Chapter 1.

Exercise 3.1 What business are we in?

When Ted Levitt addressed this question in 'Marketing myopia', he argued that the railways got into difficulty and began to decline because they became preoccupied with the technology and systems of railways, and failed to recognize the competitive threat posed by the invention of the internal combustion engine. In other words, they lost sight of the fact that the need they served was *transportation* and so failed to perceive the potential of combining the two technologies to provide an integrated road and rail service. As Levitt also observed, when a man goes into a hardware store to buy a $\frac{1}{4}$" drill he needs a $\frac{1}{4}$" hole!

To avoid the myopia described by Levitt we must first identify the generic need served – this defines the need served and the business we are in. But needs are not homogeneous and competition exists because producers develop differentiated products and services to cater to the specific wants of different customers. To define the business you are in, complete this exercise. You should spend 10–15 minutes doing this.

What is the basic need you serve?

What products/services do you sell?

What specific benefits do they offer?

Do your competitors sell other kinds of products or services? What are they?

What benefits do these other products offer?

How would you describe the customers you serve?

Exercise 3.2 How marketing orientated are you?

If you accept the marketing concept, then it is necessary to develop a marketing orientation in order to implement it. A major barrier to adopting this recommendation is that businesses comprise a number of different functions each of which tends to view the purpose of the organization from a rather different perspective. From a functional point of view marketing is probably no more or less important than any of the other major functions – research and development, engineering design, manufacturing, finance, human resource management. But a recommendation that firms become marketing orientated may be regarded by these other functions as a take-over bid by marketing which will reduce their own importance. If such differences of opinion do exist, then steps can be taken to eliminate them. This exercise will help establish the current values and attitudes.

Below is a set of twenty-eight statements which describe attitudes which may or may not exist within the organization in which you work.

We want to know about such attitudes as they exist in your organization, from your own experience. Such attitudes will be reflected by your immediate colleagues at work. By 'your organization' we mean that part of the company for which you directly work, and not the whole company internationally.

We are very concerned that you should *express your own views*, and not *the views of any group to which you may belong. You should also express attitudes as they are, and not as you feel they ought to be, or attitudes which you hope will prevail at some future date.*

You are not allowed to say 'I don't know' – even if this is true. We want you to make the best guess you can from your knowledge of the organization.

Read each of the statements below and place a tick in the box which most closely reflects the way you feel about it.

	Strongly agree	Agree	Disagree	Strongly disagree
IN MY ORGANIZATION:				
1. The sales force is expected to sell what the factory can make.	☐	☐	☐	☐
2. There is an emphasis on short-term profits at the expense of long-term success in the marketplace.	☐	☐	☐	☐

Continued

	Strongly agree	Agree	Disagree	Strongly disagree
3. We believe customers must get what they want, even if it is rather unprofitable for the company.	☐	☐	☐	☐
4. The business is committed to a long-term strategic point of view, supported by thorough market planning.	☐	☐	☐	☐
5. We focus primarily on the bottom line and productivity, and only then on the customer and the marketplace.	☐	☐	☐	☐
6. Subjective sales-force forecasts largely determine the production process.	☐	☐	☐	☐
7. We base the price of our products on cost only, worked out by the accountants, who dictate pricing strategy almost regardless of the marketplace.	☐	☐	☐	☐
8. Research and engineering are the heart of the business and our marketing people are not usually involved in determining what products we should make.	☐	☐	☐	☐
9. The factory floor is the focal centre of the organization.	☐	☐	☐	☐
10. Productivity improvements often result in changes to product specification which make the product difficult to sell to the customer.	☐	☐	☐	☐
11. Capital investment decisions which involve new technology and the relocation of manufacturing plant rarely involve the marketing people.	☐	☐	☐	☐

Continued

	Strongly agree	Agree	Disagree	Strongly disagree
12. We believe that selling volume comes first. Profits then generally follow.	☐	☐	☐	☐
13. We believe in the principle of managing the marketplace, by expecting – and managing – change.	☐	☐	☐	☐
14. We tend to fit our forecasts to the profits that we know are expected of us; then we plan how to achieve the forecast.	☐	☐	☐	☐
15. We don't pay a lot of attention to market research.	☐	☐	☐	☐
16. Product planning takes place on the factory floor, not in the marketing department.	☐	☐	☐	☐
17. Product costs, consumer prices and the whole panoply of customer-service expenditure tends to be based on profit needs, not market needs.	☐	☐	☐	☐
18. We tend to see ourselves as manufacturers rather than as marketers.	☐	☐	☐	☐
19. Our R&D people don't spend much time talking to the sales and marketing people.	☐	☐	☐	☐
20. If customers aren't happy with our products, we tend to go looking for new customers rather than new products.	☐	☐	☐	☐
21. We tend to be more concerned with return on investment in the short term, than with customer satisfaction in the long term.	☐	☐	☐	☐

Continued

	Strongly agree	Agree	Disagree	Strongly disagree
22. Our focus is on the marketplace: identifying customer needs and meeting those needs – profitably.	☐	☐	☐	☐
23. Our sales people are given great freedom in pricing, servicing and credit terms.	☐	☐	☐	☐
24. The product is the concern of our technical people, with little input from the marketing people.	☐	☐	☐	☐
25. The emphasis is on a balance between market share, market status and long-term profitability.	☐	☐	☐	☐
26. Marketing guidance for the engineers and the production people is often weak or non-existent.	☐	☐	☐	☐
27. We work with a lot of information feedback systems from the marketplace to measure and guide our activities.	☐	☐	☐	☐
28. We tend to over-engineer our products way past the point of customer need – and his or her ability to pay.	☐	☐	☐	☐

Interpretation

Earlier in this chapter we provided a wide selection of definitions of marketing. One of the most succinct of these that defines the marketing concept was that proposed by Peter Drucker (1954):

> The whole business seen from the point of view of its end result, that is from the point of view of the customer.

A similar view is contained in Levitt's exhortation that we define our business in terms of the need served. However, our interpretation of this exhortation is likely to be modified by our background and experience. In other words, we may have a different orientation and this will influence the way in which we seek to run the business. Analysis suggests that there are five basic orientations – technology, product, sales, financial and marketing. The key features of these different orientations are summarized below.

Technology orientation

● Emphasis is on research and engineering *per se*, with little recognition of economic considerations.
● Market criteria to guide research and development are inadequate or non-existent.
● The product is considered the responsibility of the technical organization, with little product planning influences from marketing.
● There is a tendency to over-engineer products to satisfy internal inclinations or even whims, beyond what the customer needs or is willing to pay for.
● Basic development, product, and facility decisions are often made between engineering and manufacturing management, without marketing participation.

Product orientation

This is the classic orientation in economies where demand exceeds supply.

● The factory floor is considered to be the business.
● The focus and emphasis are on making products.
● Little attention is given to marketing research and product planning.
● There is a tendency to base price on cost and cost alone, with value and competitive considerations largely ignored.
● Cost-reduction efforts may sacrifice product quality, product performance and customer service.
● The role of the sales organization is to sell whatever the factory chooses to make.
● If customers aren't happy, the salespeople are told to go out and get some new ones.

Sales orientation

Often confused with marketing orientation.

● The focus is on volume, not on profit.
● The prevailing point of view is that customers should be given whatever they want.
● There tends to be weak linkage between true customer needs and wants and the planning of products to be offered.
● Pricing, credit, and service policies tend to be loose.
● Production scheduling is over-influenced by subjective estimates from the field force.
● Market guidance of engineering and manufacturing is commonly inadequate.

Financial orientation
- The emphasis tends to be on short-range profit at the expense of growth and longer-range profit.
- Budgeting and forecasting frequently pre-empt business planning.
- Efficiency may outrank effectiveness as a management criterion.
- Pricing, cost, credit, service and other policies may be based on false economy influences and lack of marketplace realism.
- The business focus is not on the customer and market but on internal considerations and the numbers.

Marketing orientation
The basic features of this orientation are:

- The focus is on the marketplace – customers, competitors and distribution.
- A commercial intelligence system monitors the market.
- It requires recognition that change is inevitable, but manageable in the business arena.
- The business is committed to strategic business and marketing planning, and to creative product planning.
- The emphasis is on profit – not just volume – with growth and profit kept in balance.

Using the above descriptions it is possible to classify each of the twenty-eight statements in Exercise 3.2 as reflecting one or other of these orientations. In our judgement, these are as shown in the completed exercise which is to be found in Appendix A. In addition to classifying each statement, we have also inserted what we think would have been the answer of a marketing-orientated person. Careful consideration of the various attitude statements should make it clear what are the distinctions between the various orientations and what steps would be necessary to develop a marketing orientation.

Based on evidence from other research as well as our own direct experience in working with major corporations, six propositions must be accepted if the marketing concept is to work:

1 The idea must be an active working principle at all levels.
2 All decisions must be preceded by the question: Will our decision affect our customers?
3 Opinions about customers' views will no longer do. We must have facts.
4 As we have always planned expenditures, now we must also plan revenues.
5 Loyalty to the company and the product is not as important as loyalty to the customer.
6 Acceptance of the concept is no substitute for creating the functions and systems to ensure that it works.

Some elaboration of these propositions will be helpful in making clear what is necessary to develop as marketing orientation. (These were developed by the author in collaboration with his colleague Jack Bureau.)

The idea must be an active working principle at all levels

- All the executive officers of the corporation (the boardroom) must accept it to enable the rest to follow.
- All departments must be trained in its principles.
- Existing market functions – sales and distribution, etc. – may also have to be trained to accept it.
- The most effective organizations have found that the workforce perform better if they can accept the principle.
- Marketing must be seen to have priority in the event of functional clashes.

All decisions must be preceded by the question: 'Will our decision affect our customers?'

- The answer will frequently be 'no', but the question must be asked.
- It is generally better to ask it of the marketing people.
- When there is reasonable doubt, it may be wise to ask the customer, directly or indirectly.
- Image is as important to the customer as actuality: As long as customers *think* the decision will affect them, it does!

Opinions about customers' views will no longer do, we must have facts

- The acceptance of the marketing concept should result in the creation of a marketing research budget.
- However experienced the decision maker, he or she will be wrong about the user at least two or three times in ten.
- Without marketing research data, the chief executive always knows best.
- With marketing research data, the number of bad decisions is reduced, as well as the number of arguments.
- But research does not eradicate error.
- Nor does it often emerge with unknown facts: it tends to give precision to suspected facts.

Loyalty to the company and the product is not as important as loyalty to the customer

- To love the product you have created is human, to assume it can exist forever without change is bad judgement, to underpin the failing product with more money is stupidity.
- When a wise organization creates a brilliantly successful new product, it should immediately create the next brilliant new product which will destroy the first one.
- If the customer thinks the product is good, it's good. If the customer thinks the product is poor, it's poor. Educating customers to change their minds is usually a matter of throwing away good money: leave that to the government.
- It is better to lose face by labelling a failed new product as such, than to support it in the hope that it will, after all – and despite the evidence – succeed.

Acceptance of the marketing concept is no substitute for creating the functions and systems to ensure that it works

- Marketing will not happen by putting the label 'Marketing' on the sales manager's door.
- The marketing concept normally gets accepted along with the need for new people.
- The new people and the new concept usually puts someone's nose out of joint. You can't have new systems without changing existing practices.
- There are no inexpensive marketing managers: only substitutes for good ones.
- The new concepts, together with the new people and the new systems, cannot make the necessary changes quickly in the organization: it takes two or three years to make it happen.

From the above definitions you should be able to identify which orientation is associated most closely with each of the attitude statements. To check out your answers, turn to Appendix A at page 199–203, which summarizes the answers a marketing-orientated manager would be expected to make as well as classifying the statements by functional orientation.

Finally, Wilson and Gilligan (1997) offer the following comments on developing a marketing orientation:

> Developing marketing orientation is a long-term process and needs to be thought of as a form of investment. To a large extent this investment is in changing the organization's culture so that common values relating to the need to highlight service to customers, a concern for quality in all activities, and so forth are shared throughout the organization. This is not an appropriate target for the 'quick fix'. Steps to be taken in order to enhance an enterprise's degree of marketing orientation are:
>
> 1 Secure top management support since a bottom-up approach would be doomed from the outset given the company-wide implications of marketing orientation.
> 2 Specify a mission relating to the development of marketing orientation. This should have a plan associated with it, and the necessary allocation of resources to enable it to be executed.
> 3 A task force should be set up as part of the plan to bring together managers from across the company (and consultants who can help considerably) to carry out tasks such as:
>   - identifying the current orientation of the company;
>   - carrying out a training needs analysis as a basis for a management development programme to change the company's culture in a desired way;
>   - advising on structural changes within the company to support marketing activities;

- ensuring commitment to change via the system of rewards (such as bonuses and promotion) that will apply to facilitate change.
4 Maintain the momentum of change by means of continuous monitoring of marketing performance to ensure that inertia does not set in. Progress towards improved marketing orientation can be measured by regularly asking questions of the following type:
  - Are we easy to do business with?
  - Do we keep our promises?
  - Do we meet the standards we set?
  - Are we responsive?
  - Do we work together?

The last of these is the broadest and highlights the concern the enterprise has with satisfying its customers via the adoption of the marketing concept. Marketing orientation is concerned with implementing the marketing concept and, as such, is action oriented. However, rather than seeing it as a set of activities it is more helpful to think of marketing orientation as a process by which an enterprise seeks to maintain a continuous match between its products/services and its customers' needs. With a little elaboration we can build this into a formal definition:

Marketing orientation is the process by which an enterprise's target customers' needs and wants are effectively and efficiently satisfied within the resource limitations and long-term survival requirements of that enterprise.

Chapter 4

Marketing and competitive success

Introduction

In the preceding chapter we first set out to define the firm's business in terms of the needs which it serves rather than in terms of the products or services it offers for sale. It was contended that defining the firm's business in this way is at the very heart of a marketing orientation which we distinguish from a number of other functional orientations which may be identified in some businesses.

In proposing that a marketing orientation should underpin and drive a firm's strategy we were concerned to emphasize that such an orientation is not the preserve of the marketing department alone nor is it solely the responsibility of the marketing function. Indeed, the whole point about a marketing orientation is that it is a state of mind or a philosophy of business which should guide the firm's every action. In this sense marketing is everybody's business. That said, as a discrete business function marketing has its own contribution to make to the overall competitive success of the organization. It would seem reasonable to expect that if the activities subsumed within the marketing function are sufficiently important to justify the recommendation that firms become marketing orientated, then some evidence should be produced to justify this position. In this chapter we seek to provide such evidence.

Marketing and competitiveness

Given that during the nineteenth century Britain was the world's largest trading nation, it is inevitable that with increased international competition its share of world trade should have declined consistently since then. However, such a decline does not necessarily point to a decline in economic performance or a fall in standard of living. Clearly, the average British citizen at the end of the twentieth century is immeasurably better off than they were at the end of the nineteenth century.

A country's share of world trade is one of several measures used to assess national competitiveness. A second familiar measure is that of import penetration and the amount of goods a country exports: the balance of trade. In the case of Britain, this has caused concern for many years and continues to do so.

Both share of world trade and the balance of trade are subject to a number of criticisms as measures of competitive performance. With respect to a nation's share of world trade, it has been argued that any decline may not be due to a decline in export performance, but rather because of more and more countries participating in world trade, thereby reducing anyone's share of it. Likewise, increasing import penetration experienced by a country need not necessarily mean decline if it reflects its increasing participation in world trade. In any case, it could be argued that both these measures are subject to government policy regarding interest and exchange rates and therefore are not *only* the direct result of the competitiveness of a nation's business community.

A third measure is that of export growth, which attempts to measure the real increase, if any, in a nation's exports. As this is a largely non-comparative way of looking at a nation's exports, it avoids the criticisms levelled at both the trade balance and share of world exports as reasonable indicators of a country's competitiveness. That said, assessing anything in a vacuum is less than satisfactory.

The fourth measure of national competitiveness is manufacturing industry's share of total output; this measure is the subject of much controversy. On the one hand are those who condemn the relative decline in a nation's manufacturing sector and the growth of the service sector. The main arguments deployed by this school of thought are that as services are less tradable than manufacturers they cannot hope to pay for imported goods. Further, services ride on the back of manufacturing and yet they cannot exist without the latter.

Counter to these views, those who promote the growing service sector would argue that trade in services is increasing so that manufacturing's share of output is bound to decrease. They also point to the fact that services are tradable and that the extent to which this is so is likely to grow. Finally, service industries can buy in the goods that they require in their operations and global sourcing has become a fact of life.

While the debate about the use of these four measures of national competitiveness will smoulder on – each with its peculiar advantages and drawbacks – if a nation falls foul of all four (as is the case of Britain) it is necessary to look at its industrial performance in greater detail. By the end of the 1970s the need for such an examination had become acute and since that time both government and the private sector have expended enormous effort on seeking to identify the sources of competitive success and promoting these in all kinds and at all levels of industry. It was against this background that in 1981 the National Economic Development Office concluded that: 'Lack of expertise in marketing is the single most important cause of the disappointing performance of British companies in the last two decades.'

Since that time and given the emphasis upon *marketing* as a source of competitive success and the stress placed upon the need for firms to adopt the marketing concept and become marketing *orientated*, we are entitled to inquire why our competitive performance has not improved. Is marketing a panacea for all competitive ills, or is it just a placebo, a belief in which may provide temporary relief to the symptoms but do nothing to address the underlying causes of declining competitive health? These questions provided the background to a major piece of research undertaken by Baker and Hart, published in 1989 as *Marketing and Competitive Success*.

In our book Susan Hart and I set out first to define the nature and sources of competitiveness before seeking to identify what appeared to be the major secular trends in international competition following the end of the Second World War. In turn, this led us to identify what factors appeared to be important in achieving competitive success and, specifically, what role marketing played among these.

A review of the competitiveness literature indicated that there are at least five 'sets' of factors that influence success: environmental, organizational, strategic, managerial, and marketing. These are illustrated in Figure 4.1.

Readers requiring the full detail of this study must refer to the original book, although a short summary of it is reproduced in *Marketing Strategy and Management* (pp. 40–42). In essence, the procedure followed was to identify what constituted critical success factors (CSF) in each of the five sets of factors which impact upon overall business performance. Chief executive officers in a sample of both growth and mature or declining industries, representing both more successful and less successful firms within each of these industries, were then invited to evaluate these critical success factors.

In broad terms, three categories of factors were defined: attitudinal, strategic, and tactical. In much simplified terms, attitudinal factors are subsumed within the firm's overall orientation. Strategic factors are seen as containing two major dimensions – the company mission, and strategic marketing plans and objectives. With regard to tactical marketing factors five main areas were identified: market research and market segmentation, product policy, sales and service policy, promotional policy, and pricing policy.

In later chapters much more focused attention is given to the identification of critical success factors in each of these areas. At this juncture, however, you are invited to evaluate three sets of critical success factors that were administered to the executives participating in the survey.

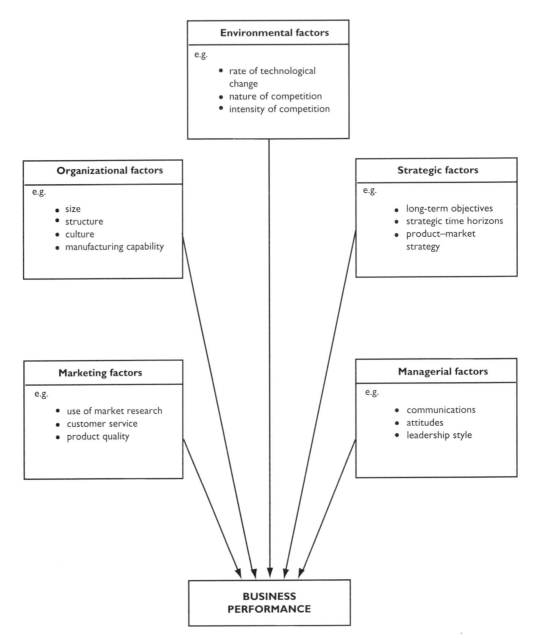

Figure 4.1 Factors influencing competitive success

Exercise 4.1 Competitive critical success factors

Analysing competitive advantage is but a means to an end, the end being how to improve on your performance and success. This exercise is a self-help diagnosis of corporate competitiveness and gives a benchmark for evaluating your company's competitiveness against standards of excellence, as understood by experts in this field. It is useful in identifying and prioritizing any areas of potential weakness within the company where there is scope for improvement.

The checklist given on page 56 is not a test, rather it provides guidance on diagnosing the degree of competitiveness of any company as it operates today because each factor permits a different aspect of competitiveness to be evaluated. To obtain maximum benefit from it you should view it both in terms of its constituent elements and its entirety.

This checklist is suitable for completion by both individual managers and group management teams. On an individual basis, you should review the elements of competitiveness in the light of your own company and past experience. If you don't work for a company, use the Barnstaple Company case study as the basis for rank ordering the product factors. The other two lists are independent of any particular industry – it is your general knowledge and judgement which is being assessed here. As such, you will be clarifying in your own mind the dynamics of competitiveness. In a management team situation (comprising members of various divisions of the company) individuals' background will influence the perception and understanding of the importance of elements on the checklist. In the group discussion, the amalgamation of experience and differing viewpoints normally results in a more balanced decision being taken on the importance assigned to each factor by the team.

In most cases it should be obvious what are good answers and what are less good. If you want to deceive yourself (or others) by cherry-picking, the only person likely to lose by this is yourself.

Rank ordering the CSF

For this exercise you are required to rank order three sets of critical success factors which prior research has shown to be particularly important in influencing a firm's competitiveness – factors associated with the product and its performance; factors influencing the design and development of new products; and management factors.

You should read through the lists carefully and then place the factors in order of importance, assigning 1 to the most important factor, 2 to the second most important factor and so on. Enter your ranking in column 1 of the three 'score' sheets.

If you are working alone, turn to page 206, where you will find the experts' ranking for each of the three sets of CSF and enter these in column 3. Now complete column 4 by inserting the arithmetic difference between your ranking (column 1) and the experts' ranking (column 3). It doesn't matter if your ranking is higher or lower, it's just the difference which matters. Sum these differences and turn to page 203 for an interpretation of your results.

If you are working as a member of a team, complete column 1 with your rankings, then arrange to meet with other team members to work out a joint ranking for each of the factors. The team scores should be entered in column 2 and the experts' rankings (page 206) in column 3. Complete columns 4 and 5 by inserting the differences between the individual and expert rankings and group and expert rankings respectively. Sum the scores and turn to page 203 for an interpretation of the results.

Product factors influencing competitiveness	Stage 1 – Individual ranking	Stage 2 – Team ranking	Stage 3 – Experts' ranking	Stage 4 – Difference between stages 1 and 3	Stage 5 – Difference between stages 2 and 3
a. Style/fashion					
b. Durability					
c. Flexibility and adaptability of the product in use					
d. Parts availability and cost					
e. Attractive appearance/shape					
f. Technical sophistication					
g. Performance in operation					
h. Ease of use					
i. Sale price					
j. Safety in use					
k. Reliability					
l. Ease of maintenance					
m. Quality of after-sales service					
n. Efficient delivery					
o. Advertising and promotion					
p. Operator comfort					
				Total	Total

Management factors influencing competitiveness	Stage 1 – Individual ranking	Stage 2 – Team ranking	Stage 3 – Experts' ranking	Stage 4 – Difference between stages 1 and 3	Stage 5 – Difference between stages 2 and 3
a. Willingness to enter into collaborative arrangements					
b. Readiness to carry out in-depth research before entering new markets					
c. Readiness to adopt modern techniques (e.g. CAD, CAM, FMS, robotization, quality circles, etc.)					
d. Readiness to look far ahead into the future					
e. Close co-operation between research and development, production and marketing					
f. Effective management of design and innovation					
g. Effective use of ideas derived from the market					
h. Effective use of ideas derived from technology					
i. Clear objectives					
j. Top management support					
k. Government support					
				Total	Total

Factors influencing the design and development of new products	Stage 1 – Individual ranking	Stage 2 – Team ranking	Stage 3 – Experts' ranking	Stage 4 – Difference between stages 1 and 3	Stage 5 – Difference between stages 2 and 3
a. The authority/power of the person directing a project					
b. The product has a higher technological content than rival product offerings					
c. Close interaction with customers/users during the stages of design and development					
d. Continuous product reviews during and after product design and development in the light of changes in the environment					
e. Extensive use of new and improved manufacturing techniques					
f. Product is designed and developed by a team of qualified engineering and industrial designers					
g. Designers see the product through to commercialization					
				Total	Total

Chapter 5

The marketing appreciation

Introduction

In the preceding chapters we have been concerned with a number of fundamental questions that need to be addressed before a strategic marketing plan can be developed. Now that you have defined the business you are in and understand the nature of a marketing orientation and its potential contribution to competitive success, it is possible to get to grips with the first of our four basic questions – 'Where am I now?'. To answer this question a comprehensive analysis of the current situation or what the military strategist would call an *appreciation* must be undertaken. In business this is often referred to as a *marketing audit*.

One of the first extended discussions of the marketing audit was written in 1959 for the American Management Association in which the author, Abe Schuchman, defined a marketing audit as:

> a systematic, critical and impartial review and appraisal of the total marketing operation: of the basic objectives and policies and the assumptions which underlie them as well as the methods, procedures, personnel and organization employed to implement the policies and achieve the objectives.

This definition focuses mainly on the internal operations of the organization. More recent definitions would extend this to include all elements of the task environment, including markets, customers, competitors, marketing intermediaries (distribution channels and dealers), suppliers and what may be called 'facilitators', that is, other organizations or agencies which facilitate the marketing process. This latter category would include the provision of financial, communication, information, and transportation services, as well as consultancy, marketing research, advertising, and so on.

In our view, this much extended evaluation goes far beyond the conventional idea of an audit, and it is for this reason that we prefer the term 'appreciation', which we see as comprising three major components:

1 A *macroenvironmental* analysis
2 A *microenvironmental* analysis
   ● industry/market
   ● competitor
   ● customer
3 Self-analysis.

We deal with each of these in turn.

Macroenvironmental analysis

Macroenvironmental analysis seeks to provide 'information about events and relationships in a company's future environment ... which would assist top management in its tasks of charting the company's future course of actions'. Environmental analysis or scanning is responsible for three major activities:

1 Generation of an up-to-date database of information on the changing business scene.
2 Alerting management to what is happening in the marketplace, the industry and beyond.
3 Disseminating important information and analyses to key strategic decision makers and influencers within the organization.

In establishing a formal environmental analysis function certain key criteria must be satisfied. First, environmental trends, events and issues must be reviewed on a regular and systematic basis. In order to do this it is important that explicit criteria are established with which the likely impact of the monitored environmental trends may be evaluated. Because it is a formal activity it should be guided by written procedures and responsibility for the implementation of these procedures must be clearly assigned. Experience indicates that scanning reports, updates, forecasts and analyses have greater impact when documented in a standardized format and when such documentation is generated on a regular basis and disseminated to predetermined personnel according to a timetable.

Where environmental scanning is embedded in a corporate strategy-making unit, it is likely to be charged with the responsibility of monitoring, forecasting and interpreting issues, trends and events which go far beyond the customer, market and competitive analyses that many firms perform as a matter of routine. It may be expected to provide a broad but penetrating view of possible future changes in the demographic, social, cultural, political, technological and economic elements of the business environment. Its purpose may then be to arm the firm's strategic decision makers with information and analyses and forecasts relevant to the strategies and plans which govern how the firm is to respond to a changing business environment. It should also provide a basis for questioning the assumptions which underpin the firm's strategic thinking and for generating new assumptions.

It is clearly important to look further afield than the task environment and Table 5.1 gives a framework for the analysis for the wider business environment.

Table 5.1 A framework for environmental analysis

Cultural	Including the historical background, ideologies, values and norms of the society. Views on authority relationships, leadership patterns, interpersonal relationships, nationalism, science and technology.
Technological	The level of scientific and technological advancement in society. Including the physical base (plant, equipment, facilities) and the knowledge base of technology. Degree to which the scientific and technological community is able to develop new knowledge and reapply it.
Educational	The general political climate of society. The degree of concentration of political power. The nature of the political organization (degrees of decentralization, diversity of functions, etc.). The political party system.
Legal	Constitutional considerations, nature of the legal system, jurisdictions of various governmental units. Specific laws concerning formation, taxation and control of organizations.
Natural resources	The nature, quantity and availability of natural resources, including climatic and other conditions.
Demographic	The nature of human resources available to the society; their number, distribution, age and sex. Concentration of urbanization of population is a characteristic of industrialized societies.
Sociological	Class structure and mobility. Definition of social roles. Nature of social organization and development of social institutions.
Economic	General economic framework, including the type of economic organization – private versus public ownership; the centralization or decentralization of economic planning; the banking system; and fiscal policies. The level of investment in physical resources and consumption.

Source: Baker (1994) adapted from Kast and Rosenweig (1974).

A survey undertaken in the 1980s of US corporations indicated that formal environmental analysis resulted in:

1 Increased general awareness by management of environmental change.
2 Better strategic planning and decision making.
3 Greater effectiveness in government matters.
4 Better industry and market analysis.
5 Better results in foreign businesses.
6 Improvement in diversification, acquisitions and resource allocation.
7 Better energy planning.

In other words, an all-round improvement in performance.

To make an effective contribution to the commissioning of an environmental scanning system, top management should attempt to establish a procedure by means of which the following parameters can be defined and redefined from time to time as circumstances dictate:

- The boundaries of both the task and the wider business environment.
- The appropriate time horizon for future studies.
- The allocation of responsibility for environmental scanning.
- The degree of formality circumscribing environmental scanning.

To define the boundaries of the firm's environments in terms of concrete measures is an almost impossible task for all but the smallest of one-product, one-customer firms. Nevertheless, the environmental scanner needs practicable guidelines by means of which he or she is able to separate relevant from irrelevant environmental information. In theory, the clearer the definition of the environment (i.e. the search domain), the clearer should be the nature of the information collected.

This exercise module is designed to enable you to identify the major environmental opportunities and threats which are likely to affect your firm over the next few years. It is not a substitute for the detailed and complete environmental analysis required to prepare strategic marketing plans. But it will permit you to develop an understanding of high priority issues which can then be the focus of more detailed research, information gathering and analysis.

The importance of macroenvironmental analysis is that it defines the threats and opportunities facing the firm, both now and in the future. Further, the macroenvironment is essentially the same for all firms and all industries and so defines the boundaries and parameters within which competition at the micro level takes place. Because of its importance we have included three complementary exercises – PEST, QUEST and ETOM.

PEST analysis

The framework for undertaking an environmental analysis was suggested in Table 5.1 and comprised nine discrete elements. For most purposes, however, a much simpler approach using four elements is used and easily remembered by the acronym PEST, standing for **P**olitical, **E**conomic, **S**ociological and **T**echnological. Each of these main elements is capable of wide definition and it is up to the analysts to decide how broadly or narrowly they wish to define them. An obvious factor influencing this decision is the organization's size and the scope of its activities. For the small organization, operations may be restricted to a *local* neighbourhood and the scope of its environmental analysis will be similarly restricted. Larger organizations may operate at a *regional* or *national* level, with very large organizations operating at the *international* or *global* level. However, it must be remembered that while the extent of the analysis will be affected significantly by organizational size its *content* will remain essentially the same on the basis that global trends impact on international/national trends which, in turn, have a major bearing on regional or local trends. Below are suggested some of the more important factors that should be considered when undertaking a macroenvironmental analysis. It is up to you to decide which to include and what level of detail is appropriate for your organization.

Political factors

Political factors are usually considered first because they influence and often determine the economic, social and technological factors. Politics controls both internal and external relations and determines a country's basic economic policies, the balance between public and private ownership and the degree of central control exercised over the organization's actions. Politics also determines social policy and through it education, employment, health, welfare, etc. Obviously politics will have a major influence on a firm's strategy. Among the main factors to be considered may be included:

International
- ideological beliefs and tensions between them.
- relations between the country where the organization is based and other countries.
- trade groupings and trade relations.
- policies on immigration, employment and emigration.

National or local
- basic ideology and the balance between free enterprise and central control.
- overall political stability.
- trade policy with regard to imports, exports and exchange control.
- fiscal policies.
- education policy.
- employment policy.
- health and welfare policies.

● regional development policy.

Economic factors

Economic factors probably have the most direct effect upon the organization in that they determine the nature and degree of competition, incentives for wealth creation, the prosperity and purchasing power of the population, the availability or otherwise of foreign exchange, etc. For purposes of analysis it is usual to distinguish between long-term and short-term factors. At the national level, the most important of these are:

Long-term
● The general level of economic activity as indicated by the stage of development reflected by its infrastructure and the proportions of persons employed in primary, secondary and tertiary industries.
● The skills, availability and costs of its labour force.
● Market potential.
● Demographic structure.
● Availability of factors of production – land, labour and capital.
● Distribution of wealth and taxation levels.

Short-term
● Phase in the business cycle.
● Inflationary or deflationary tendencies.
● Interest rates.
● Balance of payments.
● Tax levels.

Economic analysis should start with your own country and then be extended to other countries with which the organization has dealings as buyer and/or seller.

Social factors

Social factors influence the organization both externally and internally in that they determine the structure of society and the patterns of behaviour which are acceptable to the people who comprise that society. In turn, these values will have a major bearing upon both politics and economics. Among the more important social factors may be numbered:

● cultural traditions;
● class structure;
● family structure;
● attitudes to consumption and patterns of spending;
● attitudes to work and money;
● attitudes to gender;
● racial, language and religious differences;

● ethnocentrism (degree to which people are inward- rather than outward-looking). Clearly, each of these factors is capable of considerable subdivision, so that it is up to the analyst to decide which are most relevant and what are the most appropriate measures to capture their impact on organizational behaviour.

Technological factors

Technological factors differ from the three major categories in that technology, in the widest sense, is of the very essence of the organization. Manufacturing organizations are set up to exploit particular technologies while other organizations are invariably dependent upon technology to a greater or lesser degree in order to discharge their primary function, e.g. the modern service organization's dependency upon information technology. In turn, technological innovation is the major source of economic growth and a necessary if not sufficient condition for overall competitiveness, i.e. technology determines performance levels, which means that to compete an organization must be at the same level of technological development as its major rivals. To succeed, it should strive to develop a technological advantage over its rivals. Technological innovation may be embodied in the product itself and/or the process by which it is produced, distributed and consumed or used. Its influence is pervasive and the major source of competitive advantage. That said, technology now diffuses very rapidly indeed and needs constant improvement and upgrading if it is to remain a source of sustainable competitive advantage. In reviewing technology the major factors to consider are:

● the nature of the industry and its core technology(ies);
● the products and/or services produced;
● the processes and/or equipment involved;
● the skills and competences required to manage the technology;
● the market(s) served – do the users need education or skills to access the technology, does it depend upon other products or systems for its use?

As stressed, the above listings are only indicative of the factors which the analyst may wish to take into account in developing an overview of the present and future environment and the threats and opportunities which it may hold for the organization.

Bearing in mind the above discussion, now complete Exercise 5.1 by entering what you consider the most important issues (up to five) for each of the key PEST factors.

Exercise 5.1 PEST analysis

Political factors	Economic factors
1	1
2	2
3	3
4	4
5	5
Social factors	**Technological factors**
1	1
2	2
3	3
4	4
5	5

QUEST

QUEST is an acronym for **Q**uick **E**nvironmental **S**canning **T**echnique and offers a broad and comprehensive first approximation to environmental trends and events that are critical to strategic decisions.

Nanus (1982) defines QUEST as:

> a future research process designed to permit executives and planners in an organization to share their views about trends and events in future external environments that have critical implications for the organization's strategies and policies. It is a systematic, intensive, and relatively inexpensive way to develop a shared understanding of high priority issues and to focus management's attention quickly on strategic areas for which more detailed planning and analysis would be beneficial.

Certain key assumptions underline the QUEST technique. First, it is assumed that the individual executives in a firm have a view of the dynamics of the changing environments which face them. It is further assumed that in the aggregate these views represent the organization's understanding of its environment. However, in the absence of a technique such as QUEST it is unlikely that these separate views (assumptions) are articulated and shared. Thus, while individual executives may programme their future expectations into their decision making, there is no guarantee that their perceptions and interpretations of the same facts are known to and/or shared by their managerial colleagues. Only if there is a formal mechanism for enabling the firm's executives to share their different perceptions and interpretations will it be possible to identify any mismatch or disagreement between them. However, if any disagreement or mismatch is made explicit it will then become possible for management to negotiate a consensus on the interpretation of the information available to it and on the desired future towards which the organization is working. As with most aspects of decision making, a systematic approach within an agreed framework is likely to yield better results more quickly than would an unstructured approach. Further, given that the outcome is to be achieved through a negotiated consensus between the key managers, then such a process is more likely to instil a sense of ownership in the outcome than would separate independent evaluations. Table 5.2 summarizes the steps involved in implementing a QUEST analysis. The purpose of step 1 is to achieve an agreed start point for the scanning exercise. As noted above, the purpose is to help bring out into the open and share the collective wisdom and experience of the participants in terms of their future expectations. The actual methodology for executing a QUEST analysis is contained in steps 3 to 9 in Table 5.2.

Experience shows that the benefit of a QUEST analysis will be greatly enhanced by a review of other scenarios or projections of likely futures such

Table 5.2 QUEST: implementation

---

1 Review current environmental conditions.
2 Explain purpose and methodology.
3 Review 'futures' literature to stimulate thinking.
4 Define scope and boundaries for discussion including stakeholders and performance indicators.
5 Identify key issues.
6 Select agreed list.
7 Assess probability of occurrence.
8 Develop a cross-impact matrix (CIM).
9 Analyse CIM and develop scenarios.

---

as those contained in books such as *Future Shock* (Toffler, 1971), *Megatrends 2000* (Naisbitt and Aburdene, 1991) or the publications of the Brookings Institution or Hudson Institute. Such speculations by other futurists are both a source of useful ideas to stimulate thinking and an indication of the scope of the exercise. However, as step 4 in the sequence indicates, for a given organization operating in a particular industry and markets it is important that some limitations be placed upon the exercise so that its scope and boundaries need to be defined as do statements as to the perspective from which the analysis is to be undertaken and what criteria or performance indicators are to be used in assessing the importance and/or relevance of any identified issue. Step 5 is perhaps the most important step in the sequence, as it is the one in which the participants are invited to define what they see as the strategic or key issues facing their organization. Key issues may be defined as forthcoming developments, either inside or outside the organization, which are likely to have an important impact on the ability of the organization to meet its objectives. More simply put, key issues are those which could either make or break the organization, issues which, if well handled, will produce disproportionate benefit but which, if badly handled, could prove to be disastrous for the company. Key issues are often characterized by high opportunity costs for an organization in that they are likely to foreclose other options. Clearly, there needs to be a limit to the number of key issues and the best way to proceed is to invite each of the participants to construct their own list of, say, five and then circulate these so that the group may proceed to stage 6, which is the agreement of a select list. Once the agreed list has been prepared the participants should then assess the likelihood of probability of occurrence of each of the events contained in the key-issue analysis. This, in turn, should be summarized in a cross-impact matrix of the kind illustrated in Figure 5.1 in which the impact of each of the key issues is examined in the context of the other key issues. Finally, analysis of the cross-impact matrix should enable the group to develop scenarios which represent their own best expectations and understanding of the futures which face their own organization.

Event	Probability	1	2	3	4	5
1						
2						
3						
4						
5						

Figure 5.1 Cross-impact matrix

Exercise 5.2 Cross-impact matrix

Based on the above description, you should now complete the cross-impact matrix for your firm.

Event	Probability	1	2	3	4	5
1						
2						
3						
4						
5						

ETOM (environmental threats and opportunities matrix)

In Exercises 5.1 and 5.2 it was suggested that you should use a list of environmental trends or other analyses based upon futures research as a basis for selecting your own short-list of key issues. Listings of this kind are to be found in books such as *Megatrends, Megatrends 2000, Future Shock, Progress in Partnership*, etc. One such listing is presented in Figure 5.2.

In reviewing the list shown in Figure 5.2 (and extending it if you wish) it is important to distinguish between factors which may be merely transient in their existence and impact and those which are real and long-term.

- CONTINUING HIGH LEVELS OF UNEMPLOYMENT IN THE OECD COUNTRIES
- THE END OF THE AGE OF BUREAUCRATIC CENTRALISM – disappearance of old-style industries, giant factories to be replaced by smaller, hi-tech units and small-scale entrepreneurs
- PUBLIC SPENDING CUTBACKS AND/OR STRUGGLES WITH PUBLIC SPENDING
- MAJOR SHIFT IN DEMOGRAPHICS – trend towards ageing population
- POLITICS IN DEMOCRATIC COUNTRIES WILL INCREASINGLY BECOME A MATTER OF CHOICE BETWEEN HARD AND SOFT OPTIONS
- CONTINUING DEBT PROBLEMS IN DEVELOPING COUNTRIES PLUS GROWTH OF AID DEPENDENCY
- GULF SEPARATING WORLD'S INDUSTRIAL NATIONS FROM DEVELOPING COUNTRIES WILL REMAIN WIDE
- SOCIAL PROBLEMS – drugs, AIDS, muggings and burglaries
- INVESTMENT WILL BE ORIENTATED TOWARDS THE SHORT TERM
- PROLIFERATION OF SMALL BUSINESSES
- DISAPPEARANCE OF 'AUTOMATIC' GROWTH IN ALL MAJOR ECONOMIES
- HEIGHTENED COMPETITION, INCLUDING THE NEWLY-INDUSTRIALIZED COUNTRIES
- COMMON PRODUCT VALUES – growing standardization of tastes internationally
- PROTECTIONIST PRESSURES IN SOME COUNTRIES
- EROSION OF PATENT PROTECTION – large number of countries generating inventions, difficulties of enforcement
- CHANGES IN FINANCIAL SERVICES
- GLOBAL CORPORATIONS AND GLOBAL COMPETITION
- CONTINUED SHORTENING OF PRODUCT LIFE CYCLES
- DECLINE IN MANUFACTURING WILL CONTINUE *VIS-À-VIS* SERVICES
- ECONOMIES OF SCALE ARE DISAPPEARING IN SOME INDUSTRIES TO BE REPLACED BY 'MASS CUSTOMIZATION'
- TRANSPORTATION WILL INCREASINGLY GIVE WAY TO COMMUNICATION
- EXTREME AND UNPREDICTABLE CURRENCY FLUCTUATIONS – inhibiting rational decision making in manufacturing, sourcing, pricing
- VOLATILITY OF BASIC COMMODITY PRICES – leading to large changes in national purchasing power
- ACQUISITION AND MERGERS AND THE GROWTH OF STRATEGIC ALLIANCES
- PRIVATIZATION PROGRAMMES

Source: Adapted and extended from Business International Corporation, *A Guide to Corporate Survival and Growth, The New Thinking*, BIC, New York, June, 1986.

Figure 5.2 New international business realities

Undertaking the environmental analysis

The objective is to complete the environmental threat and opportunity matrix (ETOM) in Exercise 5.3. Study the instructions carefully. In essence, the aim is to identify fifteen key environmental factors which will have an important influence upon your firm through to the year 2010 and to weight and rank these, and thereby arrive at an overall positive or negative score representing a net opportunity or threat for your business.

Before studying the environmental factors listed in Exercise 5.3, you should think about the specific circumstances of your own firm, division or business unit. What objectives have been set? Who are your major customers? suppliers? competitors? Are your operations merely domestic or international? Trade or foreign investment related?

You may then like to begin by thinking about all the impacts which any particular factor will have upon your firm, e.g. technological change will affect product and process, components and final goods, all functional areas of business, the nature of government policy, patterns of international comparative advantage, etc. As any factor will probably present both threats and opportunities, you will need to weigh these up to arrive at an overall conclusion.

Interpreting the results

The final score you achieve is only meaningful in comparative terms, preferably with other colleagues from your firm (although interesting contrasts can be drawn from comparisons between different companies and sectors). You will find substantial divergence in scores recorded and these should be explored in discussion. The divergence may be due to the different personalities of yourself and your colleagues completing the ETOM, or may be derived from your different positions within the firm, e.g. finance v. manufacturing v. marketing perspectives.

Even if you are unable to reconcile your differences, at the very least the outcome of this environmental analysis should be the identification of a series of key environmental issues which should be the subject of further study and forecasting. Beyond this, you should be thinking of a more formal approach to environmental scanning and analysis within your firm, requiring systematic review of environmental trends, events and issues; the assignment of clear responsibility for environmental analysis within the firm; and the generation of written reports, updates, forecasts and analyses on a regular basis.

Variations in the approach to environmental analysis

The approach outlined here assumes that you and other executives will work largely individually on the ETOM, reconvening for a plenary session to compare results, formulate conclusions and the way ahead. There are, however, ways in which the analysis could be extended if time permits, as follows:

Before the final plenary session, have a second series of evaluations, with two groups being formed from the individuals present. Each group is required to come up with an agreed overall positive or negative score (allowing for minority reports). This will facilitate a more structured discussion in the final session.

Sophistication of the analysis could be improved by providing background briefing papers, statistics, etc. for consideration by participants.

Exercise 5.3 Completing the ETOM

Individual work

A From the list of 'New International Business Realities' (Figure 5.2) or your own judgement, choose fifteen key environmental factors likely to affect your business, assuming a time horizon through to the year 2010.

Enter the factors in column 1 as economic, social and cultural, demographic, etc. as appropriate.

B Insert minus (–) or plus (+) in column 2 or 3 depending on whether the factor is considered to be a threat or an opportunity.

C Enter a weighting of 1–5 in column 4, where 1 represents a weak threat/opportunity and 5 a strong threat/opportunity.

D Rank the fifteen factors selected according to their importance for your firm, where 1 represents minor importance and 15 represents major importance (column 5).

E Column 6 is calculated by multiplying the weighted score (column 4) by the importance score (column 5). A large positive score represents a strong opportunity; and a large negative score represents a strong threat.

F Enter subtotals (+ or –) and total (+ or –) scores in column 6.

Group work

A As a group, decide upon the focus of analysis – firm, division or business unit. In large companies, it will only be meaningful if the analysis refers to the business unit.

B Again as a group, consider the list of 'New International Business Realities' (Figure 5.2) and establish whether these are economic, social and cultural, demographic, geographic, political, government and legal, technological or competitive factors.

Page 74 of the ETOM will enable each participant to record the scores of other individuals. This will be useful in the discussion of the results, and for future reference.

On page 73, enter the subtotals for economic, social and cultural factors and overall totals.

On page 74, itemize the top three ranked environmental factors identified by each participant, e.g. currency volatility, public spending cutbacks, etc.

These 'summary statistics' will indicate the degree of agreement/disagreement between you and other participants. The diagnostic benefit of the exercise depends upon how well you resolve perceived differences in reaching a consensus judgement.

Factor		1 Event/issue	2 T (–)	3 O (+)	4 Weighting (1–5)	5 Importance (1–15)	6 Impact on company strategy
Economic	1						
	2						
	3						
	4						
	5						
Subtotal							
Social and cultural	1						
	2						
	3						
	4						
	5						
Subtotal							
Demographic	1						
	2						
	3						
	4						
	5						
Subtotal							
Geographic	1						
	2						
	3						
	4						
	5						
Subtotal							
Political	1						
	2						
	3						
	4						
	5						
Subtotal							
Government and legal	1						
	2						
	3						
	4						
	5						
Subtotal							
Technological	1						
	2						
	3						
	4						
	5						
Subtotal							
Competitive	1						
	2						
	3						
	4						
	5						
Subtotal							
						Total (–) (+)	

Summary of ETOM

| Participant | Summary of top three ranked environmental factors | | |
	Description	Opportunity (+)	Threat (−)
1	1 2 3		
2	1 2 3		
3	1 2 3		
4	1 2 3		
5	1 2 3		
6	1 2 3		
7	1 2 3		
8	1 2 3		
9	1 2 3		
10	1 2 3		
11	1 2 3		
12	1 2 3		
13	1 2 3		
14	1 2 3		
15	1 2 3		

Microenvironmental analysis

Our emphasis on macroenvironmental analysis is based on the belief that the practice of marketing at the level of the individual firm is determined largely by external factors within which the firm has to operate. It is the macroenvironmental factors which govern the structure of industries and markets and the nature of competition – the microenvironment. As indicated in the introduction, analysis of the microenvironmental may be subdivided into three main elements:

- Industry/market analysis
- Competitor analysis
- Customer analysis.

We will examine each of these in turn.

Industry/market analysis

Competition exists where two or more firms seek to serve the same end-use market. Long before the emergence of modern marketing management, economists undertook a detailed analysis of the nature of competition and the basic framework for evaluating competitive behaviour was developed by industrial economists in the 1930s. The industrial economists' model, which provides the foundation for much of Michael Porter's work on competitive strategy, contains three elements – market structure, conduct and performance.

In Chapter 2 of *Marketing Strategy and Management* we describe the basic model of structure, conduct and performance and Porter's development of it in some detail. Figure 5.3 is reproduced here to remind you of the key features of the model.

The key features of this model are:

1 All firms are faced with essentially the same *basic conditions*.
2 As a result of these conditions and competition within the market, every industry develops a particular *structure*.
3 The structure of the industry determines the alternatives open to its members and, through them, their *conduct*.
4 Competition within the market determines the *performance* of individual firms.
5 The model is *dynamic*.

The model is dynamic because it recognizes that markets are open systems subject to external forces (public policy, environmental change, etc.) and to adjustment to internal forces as reflected by the feedback loops.

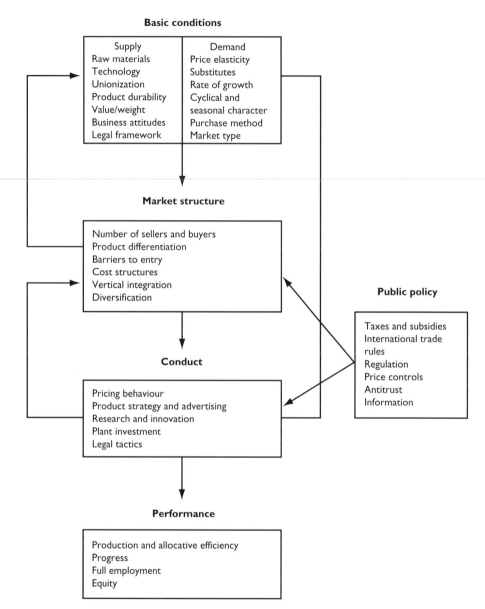

Figure 5.3 The structure–conduct–performance paradigm

For purposes of analysis economists recognize a number of competitive states which both define and are defined by structure, conduct and performance:

- monopoly;
- oligopoly;
- imperfect competition;
- perfect competition.

Monopoly and perfect competition rarely occur in the real world but are useful to define a spectrum of competitive states with oligopoly and imperfect competition lying between them. In practice competition is defined by rivalry between firms seeking to satisfy the same customer needs, i.e. it is customer needs that define the market and the nature of the firm's business.

Definition of the firm's business (Levitt, 1960) is critical to define both the boundaries/parameters of the market *and* the identity of competitors. Competitor analysis normally comprises two elements:

1 Value chain analysis.
2 Individual competitor analysis.

Value chain analysis was developed by McKinsey & Co. in the 1960s as a tool to evaluate competition based on the view that business is a system which links raw materials (supply) with customers (demand) and comprising six basic elements, as shown in Figure 5.4.

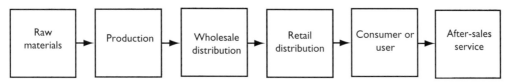

Figure 5.4 Value chain analysis

Starting with raw material extraction, the analysis proceeds by examining each major subsystem in turn in order to establish the interrelationship and interdependence between them in terms of:

1 The degree of *competition* within and between each subsystem, e.g. raw material extraction might be in the hands of only one or a few producers so that conditions are oligopolistic while retail distribution could be characterized by thousands of small sellers none of whom could influence the market. Clearly the latter circumstances describe perfect competition, and both sets of conditions apply in the oil industry. Thus in establishing the nature of competition one should measure:
   (a) the number of competitors;
   (b) their profitability;
   (c) their degree of integration;
   (d) their cost structure;
   (e) the existence and nature of any barriers to entry, e.g. technological, size of investment in production and/or marketing.
2 Where, in the total system, *value* is *added* by the activities of members of the production, distribution, or servicing subsystems. For example a significant

proportion of turnover in many consumer-durable industries is accounted for by after-sales servicing and the efficiency of this sector may have a radical influence upon the market shares of individual suppliers, as well as on industry profitability.

3 The location of *economic leverage* in the system. Does this arise from being a fully integrated producer, or can one exercise leverage by avoiding the extensive fixed investment implicit in vertical integration and concentrating on only one subsystem?

4 Where is the system's *marketing leverage*? Usually this is associated with control of a scarce resource, which might be an essential raw material, a patent on a process, control of a distribution channel, a brand name ('Hoover', 'Elastoplast') or some other type of consumer franchise.

Once the analyst has established the major characteristics of the production, distribution and servicing subsystems, the next task must be a thorough documentation of the consumer or user. Such documentation requires answers to the five basic questions which underlie all market research – who, what, where, when and how.

1 *Who* buys in terms of demographic and socio-economic criteria such as age, sex, income, education, occupation, marital status, etc. (for consumers), or status, authority, functional specialization, etc. (for users)? Who *consumes*? (Compare consumption and purchase of breakfast cereals; of hand tools in a factory; etc.)

2 *What* do people buy in terms of variety, design, quality, performance and price characteristics?

3 *Where* do people buy? In specialist outlets, in general purpose outlets, by mail or telephone from a catalogue, in the home or on their premises, i.e. how important is direct selling through representatives versus indirect selling via the media?

4 *When* do people buy? Are purchases seasonal, regular, irregular, associated with another activity, etc?

5 *How* do people buy? Impulsively, after considerable deliberation, in large quantities, small quantities, from multiple sources or a single source, etc?

A sixth and equally important question is 'Why?'. Unlike our other five questions, a definitive and factual answer cannot usually be supplied. However, when we consider that consumers (or users) do not buy products as such, but rather the satisfactions yielded by the product, then even a partial understanding of the satisfactions looked for will go a long way towards explaining actual behaviour in the marketplace.

At this juncture you should have developed a good understanding of both the company and the environment in which it is operating. It now remains to combine the two threads of the analysis in order to isolate the company's particular strengths and weaknesses in terms of the environmental threats and opportunities. An indication of the sort of questions appropriate to such a comparison is given in Figure 5.5, which is taken from McKinsey's model. This evaluation will be reinforced by the self-analysis (pages 93–8).

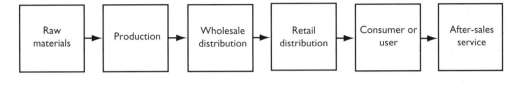

How does company compare in raw materials?
- Do they have advantages in supply?
- Degree of integration?

How does company compare in technology?
- What is their rate of product, process improvement?
- How good is process efficiency?
- Advantages in location of facilities?

How does company compare in cost and profit?
- Raw material costs?
- Processing costs?
- Profit?
- Return on investment?
- Access to capital?

How does company compare in channels?
- In which channels are company's sales concentrated?
- Do products reach point of sale faster or more efficiently?

How does company compare in distributors?
- Have they more, larger, or more effective distributors?
- Share of channel's sales?

How does company compare in economics?
- Compensation of distributors?
- Distribution costs?
- Service costs?

How does company compare in products?
- Have they greater variety, better design or quality, lower price, superior performance?
- Share of market?

How does company compare in customers?
- Who are core buyers; core consumers?
- Do these customers buy more frequently in larger quantities, or more consistently?
- How is company's product used?
- Who are core competitors?

How does company compare in service?
- Does company have a service advantage – type, quality or quantity?

How does company compare in pricing?
- Do they have price advantage (price/quality relationship)?
- Are they price leader?

How does company compare in economics?
- Service costs?
- Cost of consumer marketing?

Figure 5.5 Company's measurable strengths and weaknesses

Competitor analysis

Once you have completed the industry/market analysis it is possible to identify those firms which are in *direct* competition with your own organization and submit these to a detailed review. In this section we look at a number of approaches and techniques for achieving this. (Note: in addition to direct competitors who are offering products or services which are close substitutes for your own output, it is also useful to consider other firms with whom you may compete indirectly. For example in the market for consumer durables, furniture, floorcoverings, white and brown goods all compete with each other for the consumer's discretionary purchasing power. Such competition is indirect. For the purposes of competitor analysis we are primarily concerned with firms serving the same segment(s) as ourselves, e.g. manufacturers of washing machines, or of TVs, etc.)

Jain (1990, p. 85) suggests that in determining the degree of direct or indirect competition it is useful to look at four basic dimensions – customer need, industry competition, product line competition, and organizational competition. Table 5.3 indicates how these sources of competition may be used to identify competitive substitutes.

Table 5.3 Competitive substitutes

Customer need: liquid for the body

Existing:	Thirst
Latent:	Liquid to reduce weight
Incipient:	Liquid to prevent ageing

Industry competition (How can I quench my thirst?)

Existing industries:	Hard liquor
	Beer
	Wine
	Soft drink
	Milk
	Coffee
	Tea
	Water
New industry:	Mineral water

Product line competition (What form of product do I want?)

Me-too product:	Regular cola
	Diet cola
	Lemonade
	Fruit-based drink
Improved product:	Caffeine-free cola
Breakthrough product:	Diet and caffeine-free cola providing full nutrition

Organizational competition (What brand do I want?)

Type of firm:	Coca-Cola
	Pepsi-Cola
	Seven-Up
	Dr Pepper
New entrants:	General Foods
	Nestlé

Scope of business

Geographic:	Regional, national, multinational
Product/market:	Single v. multiproduct industry

In undertaking a competitor analysis it is important to strike a balance between essential and desirable information. Theoretically we would like to know as much about our competitors as we know about ourselves but, as we shall see when we consider the recommended scope of the *self-analysis*, realistically the time and effort involved would rarely justify this (see the discussion of the value of perfect information, pages 29–30).

It follows that the competitors for detailed review must be selected with care. It is also important to decide how serious competitors are seen to be in developing your overall strategy. George Day and Robin Wensley (1988) identify two different emphases in developing a competitive strategy, the first of which sees this focusing on rivalry with competitors and the second on concern for the customer. From these two dimensions Day creates a simple two-by-two matrix of perspectives on advantage as shown in Figure 5.6.

EMPHASIS ON COMPETITOR COMPARISONS

		Minor	Major
Emphasis on customer perspectives	Minor	Self-centred	Competitor-centred
	Major	Customer-orientated	Market-driven

Figure 5.6 Perspectives on advantage

The four 'types' of firm may be described as follows:

- **Self-centred** firms tend to be internally orientated and focus on improvements in efficiency to improve performance. Sales volume is the main external indicator and the emphasis is on market penetration. Self-centred firms survive only where there is an absence of competition, as in mature markets where there is a state of peaceful co-existence or where the firm has some form of monopoly power.
- **Competitor-centred** firms tend to predominate in mature markets with little or no growth potential where competition has become a zero sum game. Such markets are often capital-intensive with mature technologies and little opportunity for product innovation. Market penetration strategies dominate.
- **Customer-orientated** firms are frequently found in fragmented industries which are characterized by high levels of product or service differentiation leading to the existence of many segments. Under these circumstances customer satisfaction is the key indicator of performance and firms pay comparatively little attention to competitors. Product and market development are key strategies.

- **Market-driven** firms represent the norm in competitive markets where success depends upon a concern for customer needs, which drive the competitive strategy, taking into account the need to adjust this to position the firm against others which are also seeking to serve the same customer/market segments. Such firms pursue multiple strategies involving market penetration as well as market and/or product development.

Question: What kind/type of firm is yours? Why?

Given the need to develop a strategy which takes account of competitors, it follows that any analysis of them should be based upon clear views about the sources of competitive advantage. In broad terms, sources of competitive advantage may be divided into two major categories which may be defined as critical success factors and skills and competences. Critical success factors (CSF) are basically independent of the firm in the sense that they define those activities or attributes which are necessary conditions for survival in a particular market. For example in markets for fabricated materials such as steel or polymers you must be able to manufacture to agreed industry standards and specifications to be even considered a competitor in the first place. By contrast, skills and competences are particular to the firm and define its ability to satisfy the CSF and also any comparative advantage it possesses *vis-à-vis* its major competitors.

Critical success factors

The absolute number of potential CSF is large (Thompson and Strickland, 1990, identified over forty) but of these only a few are likely to be truly critical in any given competitive situation. Clearly, a key skill of the strategist is the ability to determine just what these are! Clarkson (1996) cites the work of Rockart (1979) and a group at MIT who identified four major sources of critical success factors as follows:

1 **Structure of the particular industry**   Each industry by its very nature has a set of critical success factors that are determined by the characteristics of the industry itself. Each company in the industry must pay attention to these factors. For example for the airline industry, fuel efficiency, load factors, and an excellent reservation system are held to be the most important CSFs.
2 **Competitive strategy, industry position and geographic location**   Each company in an industry is in a unique situation that is determined by its history and current competitive strategy. For smaller organizations within an industry dominated by one or two large companies, the actions of the major companies will often produce new and significant problems. A competitive strategy for the smaller firm may mean establishing a new market niche, discontinuing a product line completely, or redistributing resources among various product lines. For example in the personal computer industry, the

survival of many smaller firms depends upon the compatibility of their products with IBM. Just as differences in a firm's position within an industry dictate CSFs, differences in geographic location can lead to differing CSFs from one company to another.

3 **Environmental factors**   Changes in the gross national product, the economy, political factors, and demographics lead to changes in the critical success factors of various industries and firms. At the beginning of 1973 virtually no chief executive in the UK or USA would have listed 'energy supply availability' as a critical success factor. Following the oil embargo, however, this factor suddenly became very important. (Note also how defence requirements after 1989 have diminished.)

4 **Temporal factors**   Internal organization considerations often become temporal critical success factors. These are areas of activity that are significant for the success of an organization for a particular period of time because the activities are below the threshold of acceptability. For example if several key executives of an investment banking firm quit to form a competing 'spin-off firm', rebuilding of the executive group would become a critical success factor for the organization. The case of Saatchi and Saatchi illustrates this.

Exercise 5.4 Critical success factors

The identification of CSFs will be informed by the industry market analysis and, particularly, by the value chain analysis, which indicates where specific kinds of competitive advantage have a special significance. Once a short-list of, say, six CSF is identified, it is possible to use these for both self and competitor assessment. A factor rating table for doing this is given below. The key steps are:

1 Identify the critical success factors.
2 Rank order these in terms of importance and weight accordingly.
3 Rate your own company and its three closest/major competitors out of 10, assigning 10 for excellent performance, 7 for good, 5 for average, 3 for fair and 1 for poor.
4 Multiply the scores by the weightings and sum the scores for all those rated.
5 Diagnose the scores and set out proposals for remedial action.

Critical success factor	Weighting	Own Firm rating score	Competitor 1 rating score	Competitor 2 rating score	Competitor 3 rating score

Skills and competences

The notion of 'distinctive competence' first came into currency at the Harvard Business School in the business policy course. Selznick (1957) defined it as any factor at which a firm was uniquely good by comparison with its main competitors. Such distinctive competences may exist in any key area, as suggested by Table 5.4.

Identifying distinctive competences should be undertaken in conjunction with the value chain analysis (see page 77).

The concept of distinctive competences was further developed by Pralahad and Hamel (1990) in their analysis of factors underlying Japanese competitive success in which they identified the acquisition and exploitation of distinctive, or what they called 'core' competences, as a major source of

Table 5.4 Distinctive competence in key areas

Key area	Dimensions
Product/market	Share of existing markets Range of products Position in product life cycle Dependence upon key product for sales/profits/cash flow Distribution network Marketing and market research
Production	Number, size, location, age and capacity of plants Specialization/versatility of equipment Production and cost levels Cost/availability of raw materials Production control systems
Finance	Present asset structure Present capital structure Access to additional equity and debt finance Pattern of cash flow Procedures for financial management
Technology	Currency of production methods and products R&D spending and effectiveness
Organization and human resources	Management style and succession Staff development policies Management/labour force relationship Reward structures

Taken from Clarkson (1996).

competitive advantage. In Pralahad and Hamel's study a core competence was seen as a unique and difficult to replicate combination of a number of distinctive competences. Thus, while competitors might benchmark and match specific skills and competences it was the combination of these which conferred the *sustainable competitive advantage*. For example Pralahad and Hamel see Coca-Cola's competitive advantage arising from a combination of brand strength, distribution network and geographic spread. For Benetton it is fast cycle times, computer-aided manufacture and just-in-time dyeing while for Toyota it is just-in-time manufacturing, fast cycle times and economies of scale.

In some cases core competences evolve or 'emerge' (Mintzberg and Walters, 1985); in others they are the outcome of deliberate strategic planning. For example Pralahad and Hamel describe Canon's assault on the copier market as comprising an eight-step plan as follows:

1 Establish the strategic intent to 'beat Xerox'.
2 Identify Canon's existing core competences.
3 Understand Xerox's technology and patents to identify the necessary competences.
4 License the technology to gain market experience and develop the core competences not already possessed.
5 Invest in R&D to improve on the existing technology to acquire and start to exploit core competences, primarily to achieve cost reductions, e.g. by standardization of components, improving ease of maintenance and replenishment.
6 License out own technology to fund further R&D and thus further consolidate the core competences required to beat Xerox.
7 Open challenge with 'business warfare', first by attacking markets where Xerox is weakest – Japan, then Europe.
8 Finally, an innovative, rather than imitative, attack on markets where Xerox is strongest, e.g. by selling rather than leasing, distributing through office equipment retailers rather than direct, and focusing promotion on end-users rather than on corporate functional heads.

Exercise 5.5 Skills and competences

Bearing in mind the foregoing discussion and examples you should now seek to capture and define the organization's skills and competences. To begin with, list these using the checklist of distinctive competence in key areas (Table 5.4). Next see if you can identify any combinations or clusters of specific competences which are unique to you, difficult to copy or replicate and which are seen as a source of *sustainable competitive advantage*.

Distinctive competence

Product/market

Production

Finance

Technology

Organization and human resources

Core competences

Customer analysis

The essence of customer analysis is the determination of buyer behaviour. It lies at the very heart of developing an effective marketing strategy.

While it is commonplace to distinguish between individual and organizational buyer behaviour, our own view is that they are essentially the same. In *Marketing Strategy and Management* (1992), we develop this theme at some length and you are recommended to review the appropriate chapter before completing the exercise in this section. For those without immediate access to this source, the basic arguments are as follows.

Consumption is a response to a felt need which may be prompted by in-built stimuli (physiological) or an extrinsic cue which triggers a response based on experience or learning. It follows that *awareness* of a need is the first step in the buyer decision process. Given the number of cues or stimuli competing for our attention (awareness), we possess an in-built defence mechanism known as *selective perception* which operates at the subconscious level and only admits information to our conscious awareness when it is felt such information will satisfy a need.

On recognizing a cue or stimulus we can decide whether to consider it further (*interest*), or ignore it – at least for the time being. If consideration stimulates genuine interest, then we will evaluate both the need and the information we have about objects which may satisfy the need. Given the strength of the need and the degree of risk we perceive in making a decision, we may search for additional information.

In evaluating the information we have gathered, two criteria dominate both individual and organizational buying behaviour – *fitness for purpose* (will it satisfy the need?) and *cost benefit* (is it worth it?). Rationality requires that we will prefer the object which offers the highest perceived value. (It is important to remember that in selecting and evaluating this information subjective influences such as attitudes, opinions and emotions will all affect the decision process.)

Provided that one object clearly outperforms all the others, the decision maker will have no difficulty in reaching a conclusion. The dilemma we face is that, by definition, competition means that we will have access to closely matched alternatives in terms of both fitness for purpose and cost benefit. It follows that in discriminating between objectively near-perfect substitutes we will have to use our subjective preferences – what we term 'behavioural response' in our model of buyer behaviour.

If this simple model of buyer behaviour is correct, then it follows that sellers must define carefully both the objective needs which customers are seeking to satisfy as well as the subjective factors which may influence or modify the individual's perception of the objective factors. Table 5.5 indicates a fairly comprehensive listing of the sort of factors which need to be evaluated when undertaking a customer analysis.

Table 5.5 Customer analysis

What
benefits does the customer seek?
factors influence demand?
functions does the product perform for the customer?
are important buying criteria?
is the basis of comparison with other products?
risks does the customer perceive?
services do customers expect?

How
do customers buy?
long does the process last?
do various elements of the marketing programme influence customers at each stage of the
   process?
do customers use the product?
does the product fit into the lifestyle or operation?
much are they willing to spend?
much do they buy?

Where
is the decision made to buy?
do customers seek information about the product?
do customers buy the product?

When
is the first decision to buy made?
is the product repurchased?

Why
do customers buy?
do customers choose one brand as opposed to another?

Who
are the occupants of segments?
buys our product and why?
buys our competitors' products and why?

Exercise 5.6 Objective needs analysis

This exercise invites you to list the objective needs that your product satisfies. (Three pro formas are included in the book. If you have more than three products, photocopy additional pro formas as required.)

Product	**Rating**					
Factor	Excellent 5	Good 4	Average 3	Fair 2	Poor 1	Not applicable 0
Performance						
Reliability						
Price						
Availability/delivery						
Technical sophistication						
After-sales service						
Ease of use						
Safety						
Ease of maintenance						
Parts availability/cost						
Attractive appearance						
Others:						
Total						Overall total

Product	Rating					
Factor	Excellent 5	Good 4	Average 3	Fair 2	Poor 1	Not applicable 0
Performance						
Reliability						
Price						
Availability/delivery						
Technical sophistication						
After-sales service						
Ease of use						
Safety						
Ease of maintenance						
Parts availability/cost						
Attractive appearance						
Others:						
Total						Overall total

Product	Rating					
Factor	Excellent 5	Good 4	Average 3	Fair 2	Poor 1	Not applicable 0
Performance						
Reliability						
Price						
Availability/delivery						
Technical sophistication						
After-sales service						
Ease of use						
Safety						
Ease of maintenance						
Parts availability/cost						
Attractive appearance						
Others:						
Total						Overall total

An aggregate score (AS) should be computed for each product and then expressed as a percentage of the potential score which equals the number of factors (F) times five, i.e.

$$\text{Rating} = \frac{AS}{5F}$$

An alternative approach to computing a score is to plot information on a bar chart, as illustrated in Figure 5.7 produced by Develin & Partners.

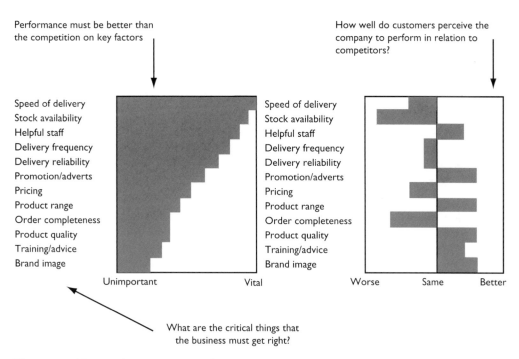

Figure 5.7 External customer needs survey

For the moment we will leave the question of subjective factors but will return to these in Chapter 6 when we discuss market segmentation.

Self-analysis

Having completed an analysis of the external microenvironment, the penultimate step in the marketing appreciation is to complete a self-analysis or what is sometimes referred to as an *internal audit*. In many respects the internal audit covers the same issues as the competitor analysis in that it is designed to identify and evaluate assets, resources, skills and competences. That said, the internal audit is likely to be much more comprehensive, if for no other reason than that one has open access to much more information. For example in the *Encyclopedia of Marketing* (Baker, 1995), Aubrey Wilson writes:

The audit commences with the collection and study of the company's documentation. This usually comprises the following, but for the individual organization there may also be specific items:

- Organization chart (official and informal).
- Corporate/market/profit plan/budgets.
- Sales analyses.
- Job specifications of marketing and sales personnel including the sales or order office.
- Catalogues and brochures (own and competitors').
- Press releases.
- Salesforce costs analyses.
- Media advertising and direct mail material including schedules and appropriations (own and competitors').
- Other marketing cost analyses.
- Salesforce reporting formats.
- Customer database formats.
- Enquiry records.
- Pricing forms including discount structure.
- Sales analyses (home and export).
- Salesforces', agents' and distributors' performance assessment forms.
- New product search reports and evaluations.
- List of journals and publications received.
- List of external statistics regularly received.
- Guarantee claim record.
- Credit note analyses.
- Complaints analyses.
- Service record formats.
- Agency contracts.
- Terms of business.
- Costing and pricing formats.

- Training programmes for sales and/or marketing people – content and frequency.
- Details on any market research and customer satisfaction undertaken or bought in during the last one or two years.

In *Marketing* (Baker, 1996) it states that:

the purpose of the internal audit is to develop a comprehensive list of the organization's resources, together with an assessment of their relative importance *vis-à-vis* each other. The audit should encompass all of the following:

1 **Physical resources**
Land
 – as a source of raw materials
 – as a location for manufacturing and distributive activities.

Buildings
 – general purpose or specific, i.e. designed for light engineering, assembly, storage, etc., or for heavy manufacturing requiring special foundations, services, etc.

Availability of and access to
 – power supplies, drainage and waste disposal
 – transportation: road, rail, canal, port facilities, etc.

Plant and equipment
 – general purpose, e.g. lathe, press
 – specific, e.g. steel rolling mill, foundry, etc.
2 **Technical resources** Essentially these reside in the technical expertise of the firm's employees, together with the possession of patents, licences or highly specialized equipment.
3 **Financial resources** These comprise the liquid assets in the firm's balance sheet, the ability to secure loans against fixed assets and the ability to raise capital in the market on the basis of past and anticipated future performance. They also comprise the skill of the firm's financial management.
4 **Purchasing resources** Managerial expertise backed by a special advantage enjoyed by the firm by virtue of its size or connections, e.g. reciprocal trading agreements.
5 **Labour resources** The skills, experience and adaptability of the work force.
6 **Marketing resources** The degree of consumer/user acceptance or 'franchise' developed through past performance. Access to and degree of control over distribution; the specialized skills and experiences of personnel.

While such an audit should provide a good summary of the nature and extent of the company's assets, together with an indication of the relative importance of the major business functions, its value can only be realized by comparison with similar data for companies with which it is competing. To obtain this one must carry out an external audit as described earlier.

The development of effective marketing strategies requires firms to match skills and competences (competitive advantages) with market opportunities.

Conventional wisdom proposes:

1 Structure follows strategy.
2 Strategy should be marketing orientated, i.e. based on customer needs.

The reality is that structure usually determines strategy and almost invariably does so in the short term. It follows that a clear definition and measurement of the firm's strengths and weaknesses is a prerequisite for strategic marketing planning.

The internal marketing audit comprises five main elements:

1 The marketing strategy audit.
2 The marketing organization audit.
3 The marketing systems audit.
4 The marketing productivity audit.
5 The marketing function audit.

The marketing strategy audit contains two main elements:

1 Identification and evaluation of the firm's *marketing objectives*.
2 Identification and evaluation of the firm's *marketing strategy* and its relationship to the declared objectives.

We return to these in the next chapter.

The marketing organization audit contains three main elements:

1 Evaluation of the *formal structure*.
2 Evaluation of the *marketing function*.
3 Evaluation of the *interface efficiency*.

The marketing systems audit is concerned with four major subsystems:

1 Marketing information.
2 Marketing planning.
3 Marketing control.
4 New product development.

The marketing productivity audit measures two major dimensions:

1 Profitability.
2 Cost effectiveness.

The marketing function audit is focused on the main elements of the marketing mix:

1 Product.
2 Price.
3 Distribution.
4 Personal selling.
5 Advertising, promotion and publicity.

In addition to the specific marketing resources, a full self-audit should also define and measure the firm's other major resources in respect of:

1 Physical – land, buildings, etc.
2 Technology.
3 Finance.
4 Procurement.
5 Personnel.

Six alternative auditing approaches are:

1 Self-audit.
2 Lateral audit, i.e. persons from different functions audit each other.
3 Audit from above.
4 Company auditing office.
5 Company task-force audit.
6 External audit.

While the intention is to measure internal strengths and weaknesses as *objectively* as possible, the important thing is to compare the firm with its competitors to form a *relative* judgement. Factor rating tables should be constructed to assist this process.

In sum, the internal appraisal should provide answers to the following questions:

● What is the company's present position?
● What is the company good at?
● What are the major problems faced?
● What is the company poor at?
● What major resources, expertise exist?
● What major resources, expertise deficiencies exist?

Putting it all together

By now you should have an excellent understanding of the major macro-environmental trends which influence all firms in all industries; of the microenvironmental forces which shape competition and particularly market structure, conduct and performance (critical success factors); of your customers' needs and expectations and your own and your competitors' strengths and weaknesses. It remains to try and synthesize all this information into a single, simplified summary statement which will provide the basis for developing your own strategy and marketing plan. The technique for achieving this is usually known as the SWOT analysis – SWOT being an acronym for **S**trength, **W**eaknesses, **O**pportunities and **T**hreats.

In discussing self-analysis we stated that developing an effective marketing strategy is essentially a matching process in which the firm seeks to identify marketing opportunities which will allow it to use its resources, skills and competences to optimum effect. While it is true that long-term survival and success depend on the ability to detect and anticipate major trends in the macroenvironment, in practice it is probably better to realize that the long term is made up of a series of short terms and in the short term it is *survival* that matters. This perspective enables us to reconcile the main schools of thought about strategic planning. While the majority of theorists and consultants extol the benefits of structured long-term strategic planning, followers of Henry Mintzberg take the view that strategy 'emerges' as the organization responds to changes in its environment. The hybrid and preferred solution is that we must have a strategy which gives an overall sense of direction and purpose for the long term. Without this, how do we know what corrective actions to take when confronted by an unforeseen or unanticipated event in the short term? In the same way that the sailor must adjust his course to allow for wind and weather beyond his control, so the manager needs to modify the long-term strategy in the light of emerging events. It is the summary or SWOT analysis which provides the basis for deciding where we are today – our strengths and weaknesses – and what future possibilities are available to us – opportunities and threats.

As noted earlier, you should have already identified the key issues and critical success factors which define the opportunities and threats in the external environment as well as your own strengths and weaknesses. What we need to do now is combine these to provide an overview of the current position and likely future events. To begin with, we provide three worksheets to focus our analysis of the external environment.

Exercise 5.7 should be familiar in that it covers the PEST analysis and up to five events/issues for each of the four major dimensions – political, economic, social and technological. What's new in the requirement is that you now classify each event/issue as a Threat (T) or Opportunity (O) and express your judgement on a scale of 1 to 10 about the likelihood of the event occurring, its importance and potential impact, where 1 is a low or negligible likelihood/importance/impact and 10 represents an almost certain likelihood, critical importance and major impact.

Paradoxically, many opportunities may represent threats and vice versa. In making your assessment you will have to decide which point of view you are going to adopt and it is here that your judgement of importance, impact, etc. will help in deciding.

Once you have completed Exercise 5.7 you should repeat the operation for the microenvironmental factors (sometimes referred to as the 'task environment') by completing Exercise 5.8 following the same basic procedure.

The results of the two environmental analyses may now be combined in Exercise 5.9, which requires you to plot the outcomes of the threats and opportunities analysis on an occurrence/impact matrix. As the name implies, this matrix combines your judgements about the likelihood of occurrence and its potential impact on the organization and so permits us to prioritize the issues calling for attention, as shown in Figure 5.8.

The second part of the SWOT analysis – the identification of strengths and weaknesses – is the product of the self-analysis completed in Exercise 5.7. Depending on the number of items you've identified it may be necessary to weight and rank order these to reduce the list to manageable proportions. The

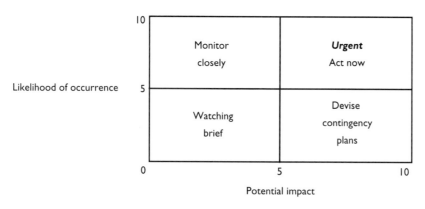

Figure 5.8 Occurrence/impact matrix

ultimate objective is to combine the internal and external analyses into a single, one-page summary as indicated in Exercise 5.10. It is this overview which provides the basis for identifying the strategic options available to the organization and the selection of a preferred strategy (the subject of the next chapter).

As with all the other exercises in the book, all the individuals responsible for developing and implementing a strategy should be required to construct their own SWOT analysis. From our earlier review of managerial orientations we would expect that the individual's perception of importance and impact will be mediated by their experience and functional responsibilities. It follows that once the individual evaluations have been compiled they need to be discussed, reconciled and a consensus reached before proceeding to the next phase.

Exercise 5.7 Macroenvironmental threat and opportunity matrix

Factor	Event/issue	Threat/ opportunity	Probability/ importance	Impact
Political	1 2 3 4 5			
Economic	1 2 3 4 5			
Social	1 2 3 4 5			
Technological	1 2 3 4 5			

Exercise 5.8 Task environment threat and opportunity matrix

Factor	Event/issue	Threat/ opportunity	Probability/ importance	Impact
Market	1 2 3 4 5			
Competitors	1 2 3 4 5			
Suppliers/ intermediaries	1 2 3 4 5			
Other value chain elements	1 2 3 4 5			

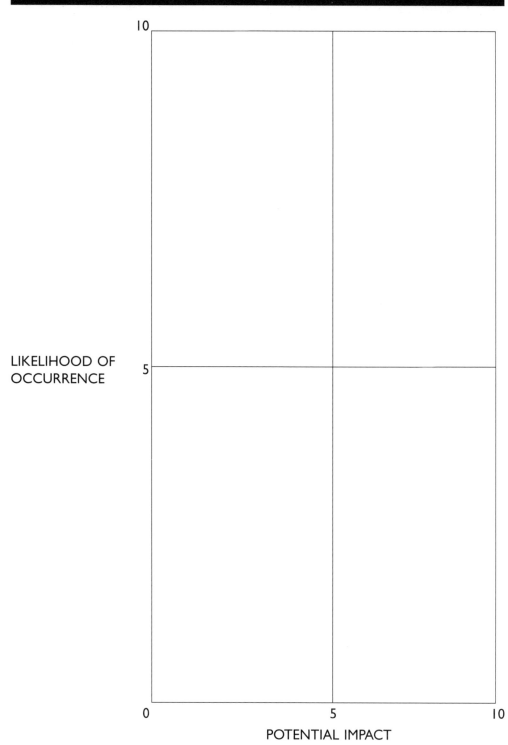

Exercise 5.9 Occurrence/impact matrix

Exercise 5.10 SWOT analysis

STRENGTHS	OPPORTUNITIES
WEAKNESSES	THREATS

Chapter 6

Where do we want to go?

Introduction

Now that you can answer the question 'Where am I now?', and have identified the current and future threats and opportunities facing you, we are ready to move into the second stage of the SMP process – deciding where we want to go.

In this chapter we look first at the basic strategic options and a number of diagnostic frameworks which will be helpful in choosing between them. In selecting a core strategy it will be necessary to confirm, or possibly modify, the firm's *mission*. This will receive explicit attention.

Given agreement on the mission and the strategic direction to be followed, the next step will be to set specific corporate objectives which will enable us to operationalize the mission. In setting objectives it will be necessary to make certain assumptions related to issues and outcomes about which we are uncertain and/or lack information. As we shall see, this is a vital step in ensuring that all the involved decision makers are agreed on the key issues and are 'singing from the same hymn sheet'.

Having established clear objectives and assumptions, we can now select a core strategy and focus on the specific marketing opportunities we wish to address through the processes of segmentation, targeting and positioning.

Strategic options

Discussion of the strategic options available to firms occupies a central place in any discussion of SMP and is the subject of extended treatment in formal courses and textbooks dealing with the subject. For the purposes of the book we summarize below some of the concepts and analytical frameworks wh we have found most useful in reducing the plethora of advice to m manageable proportions.

Faced with information overload, a key managerial skill is the ability to reduce the available data to manageable proportions. Such data reduction may be greatly facilitated by reference to two 'curves' and four 'boxes':

- The demand curve.
- The product life cycle curve.
- Ansoff's growth/vector matrix.
- The directional policy matrix.
- The Boston box.
- Baker's box.

The demand curve

The law of demand stipulates that the lower the price the greater the quantity demanded (and vice versa). This relationship is reflected in demand curves which slope downward from left to right as shown in Figure 6.1.

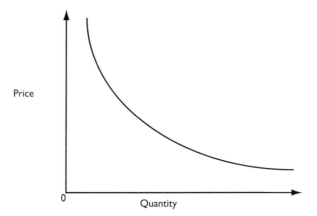

Figure 6.1 The demand curve

The demand curve represents the aggregated demand of all those individuals or organizations which have a need for the product or service in question, and the resources with which to acquire a supply. The shape of the curve is determined by the actual price intending buyers are prepared to pay, which, in turn, depends on the salience or importance of the object to purchasers and their disposable income. Consideration of the demand curve suggests two basic alternative strategies:

- undifferentiated marketing;
- differentiated marketing.

Under conditions of undifferentiated marketing it is assumed that consumers cannot discriminate significantly between the competitive offerings available, with the result that they will buy from the lowest priced source. In turn, this means the most efficient supplier will gain further economies of scale and experience, thus consolidating the cost leadership position.

In any industry, only one (monopoly) or a small number of sellers (oligopoly) are able to achieve the economies of scale which enable them to exercise cost leadership. For the vast majority of competitors survival depends on differentiating their output in some meaningful way so that buyers will be willing to pay a higher price for the additional benefits. In other words, differentiated marketing enables sellers to create a micro demand curve of their own.

Differentiation arises from innovation and innovation results in a continuous cycle of change in which new and improved solutions displace and replace less satisfactory solutions which preceded them. In marketing this phenomenon is captured in the product life cycle, or PLC.

Conventional PLCs are represented as having four phases – introduction, growth, maturity and decline – which may be plotted graphically as shown in Figure 6.2.

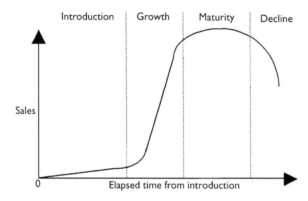

Figure 6.2 The product life cycle curve

In reality PLCs assume many different forms and this has led some commentators to dismiss the concept as lacking in practical value. This misconception arises because of a wish to use the PLC as a predictive device for forecasting and tactical planning when its true value is as a diagnostic tool which reminds us of the inevitability of change and the need for long-term strategic thinking.

The PLC concept is an analogy of the biological life cycle. Recognition of this suggests at least two different interpretations:

● Darwinian evolution through a process of gradual adaptation.
● Punctuated equilibrium in which long periods without change are disrupted by an external catalyst.

Both explanations are conceptually valuable for marketing strategists.

In addition to its value as a conceptual tool, the PLC may also be used prescriptively to suggest the most appropriate marketing mix to be used at the different stages of the product's life cycle. Tables 6.1 and 6.2 illustrate two interpretations of using the PLC concept in this way.

Table 6.1 How PLC advocates view the implications of the cycle for marketing action

Effects and response	Stages of the PLC			
	Introduction	Growth	Maturity	Decline
Competition	None of importance	Some emulators	Many rivals competing for a small piece of the pie	Few in number with a rapid shakeout of weak members
Overall strategy	Market establishment; persuade early adopters to try the product	Market penetration; persuade mass market to prefer the brand	Defence of brand position; check the inroads of competition	Preparations for removal; milk the brand dry of all possible benefits
Profits	Negligible because of high production and marketing costs	Reach peak levels as a result of high prices and growing demand	Increasing competition cuts into profit margins and ultimately into total profits	Declining volume pushes costs up to levels which eliminate profits entirely
Retail prices	High to recover some of the excessive costs of launch	High to take advantage of heavy consumer demand	What the traffic will bear; need to avoid price wars	Low enough to permit quick liquidation of inventory
Distribution	Selective as distribution is slowly built up	Intensive; employ small trade discounts since dealers are eager to store	Intensive; heavy trade allowances to retain shelf space	Selective; unprofitable outlets slowly phased out
Advertising strategy	Aim at the needs of early adopters	Make the mass market aware of brand benefits	Use advertising as a vehicle for differentiation among otherwise similar brands	Emphasize low price to reduce stock
Advertising emphasis	High to generate awareness and interest among early adopters and persuade dealers to stock the brand	Moderate to let sales rise on the sheer momentum of word-of-mouth recommendations	Moderate, since most buyers are aware of brand characteristics	Minimum expenditures required to phase out the product
Consumer sales and promotion expenditures	Heavy to entice target groups with samples, coupons, and other inducements to try the brand	Moderate to create brand preference (advertising is better suited to do this job)	Heavy to encourage brand switching, hoping to convert some buyers into loyal users	Minimal to let the brand coast by itself

Source: Dhalla, N.K. and Yuspeh, S. (1976). Forget the product life cycle concept! *Harvard Business Review*, January–February.

Table 6.2 The Arthur D. Little strategic condition matrix

Competitive position	Stage of industry maturity			
	Embryonic	*Growth*	*Mature*	*Ageing*
Dominant	Grow fast Build barriers Act offensively	Grow fast Aim for cost leadership Defend position Act offensively	Defend position Increase the importance of cost Act offensively	Defend position Focus Consider withdrawal
Strong	Grow fast Differentiate	Lower costs Differentiate Attack small firms	Lower costs Differentiate Focus	Harvest
Favourable	Grow fast Differentiate	Focus Differentiate Defend	Focus Differentiate Hit smaller firms	Harvest
Tenable	Grow with the industry Focus	Hold on or withdraw Niche Aim for growth	Hold on or withdraw Niche	Withdraw
Weak	Search for a niche Attempt to catch others	Niche or withdraw	Withdraw	Withdraw

Source: Adapted from Arthur D. Little.

Ansoff's growth/vector matrix

In developing a competitive strategy several useful frameworks have been developed which reduce the critical dimensions to two factors and then consider only two or three variations for each factor, thus creating simple matrices containing between four and nine alternatives.

One of the original and most influential of these matrices is Igor Ansoff's growth/vector matrix (Figure 6.3), which is based on two dimensions he terms mission and product.

Ansoff defined these strategies as follows:

1 Market penetration: the company seeks increased sales for its present products in its present markets through more aggressive promotion and distribution.

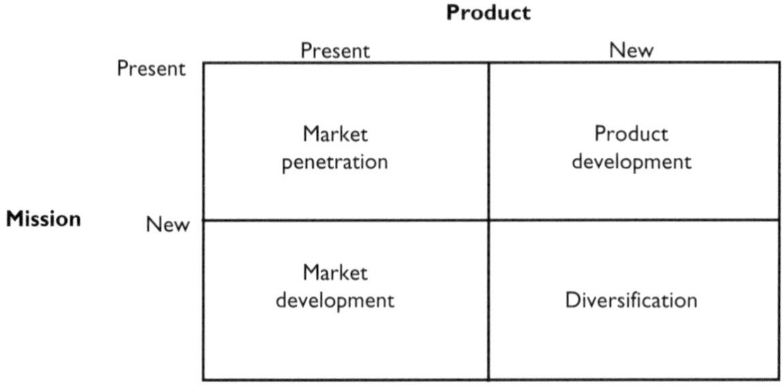

Product

	Present	New
Present	Market penetration	Product development
New	Market development	Diversification

(axis label left: **Mission**, with Present / New)

Figure 6.3 Ansoff's growth/vector matrix

2 Market development: the company seeks increased sales by taking its present products into new markets.
3 Product development: the company seeks increased sales by developing improved products for its present markets.
4 Diversification: the company seeks increased sales by developing new products for new markets.

The directional policy matrix

While Ansoff's matrix is mainly concerned with strategic choices, Shell's directional policy matrix (Figure 6.4) is more diagnostic in character and relates the company's competitive capabilities to prospects for sector profitability.

Prospects for sector profitability

	Unattractive	Average	Attractive
Weak			
Average			
Strong			

(axis label left: **Company's competitive capabilities**)

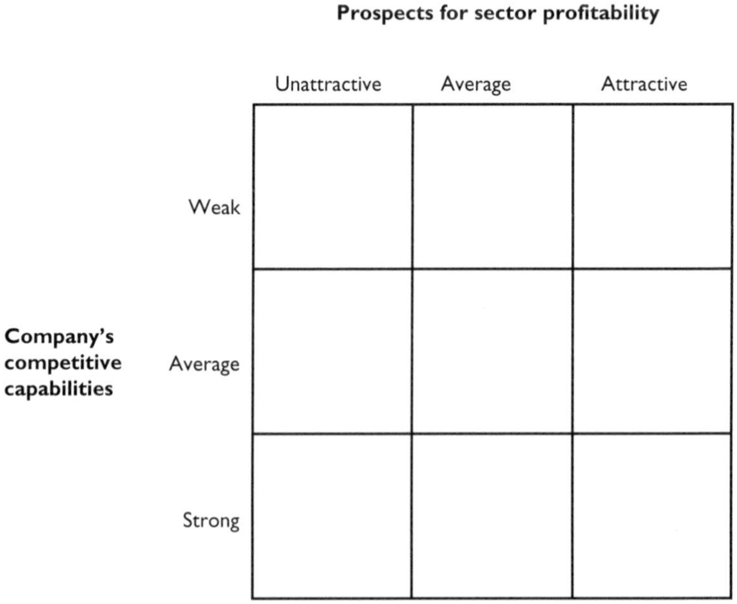

Figure 6.4 The directional policy matrix

		Strong	Medium	Weak
Market attractiveness	High	**Protect position** Invest to grow at maximum digestible rate. Concentrate effort on maintaining strength.	**Invest to build** Challenge for leadership. Build selectively on strengths. Reinforce vulnerable areas.	**Build selectively** Specialize around limited strengths. Seek ways to overcome weaknesses. Withdraw if indications of sustainable growth are lacking.
	Medium	Build selectively. Invest heavily in most attractive segments. Build up ability to counter competition. Emphasize profitability by raising productivity.	Selectivity/manage for earnings. Protect existing programme. Concentrate investments in segments where profitability is good and risk is relatively low.	Limited expansion or harvest. Look for ways to expand without high risk; otherwise, minimize investment and rationalize operations.
	Low	**Protect and refocus** Manage for current earnings. Concentrate on attractive segments. Defend strengths.	**Manage for earnings** Protect position in most profitable segments. Upgrade product line. Minimize investment.	**Divest** Sell at time that will maximize cash value. Cut fixed costs and avoid investment meanwhile.

Strong   Medium   Weak
Competitive position

Figure 6.5 Generic strategy options

In *The Marketing Book* the generic strategies shown in Figure 6.5 are suggested depending on which 'box' you find yourself in. (Note: the axes have been reversed!)

The third matrix (Figure 6.6), developed by the Boston Consulting Group, is even more focused on the products contained in the firm's portfolio and relates market growth to market share.

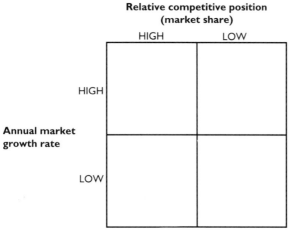

Figure 6.6 The Boston box

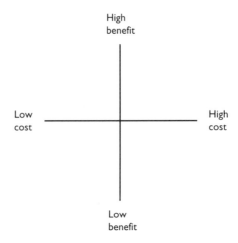

Figure 6.7 The perceptual map

An alternative to the Boston box, which is only relevant to a minority of firms with many products and measurable market shares, is to plot the firm's position *vis-à-vis* its competitors using a perceptual map.

Perceptual maps use two dimensions, with cost (price) and benefit (performance) being the most usual (Figure 6.7). Firms are then plotted according to the analyst's perception of their ratings on these two dimensions.

Baker's box

A more powerful diagnostic tool (Baker's box) may be developed as shown in Figure 6.8.

Fuller discussions of all these techniques/concepts are to be found in the list of recommended textbooks. For the purposes of the book we have developed a series of exercises to illustrate how they might be used in practice. While it will be useful to complete all the exercises in real life one would recognize that there is a considerable overlap between them (for example the Boston box is simply a representation of the PLC), and so only select those diagnostics most suited to the task in hand.

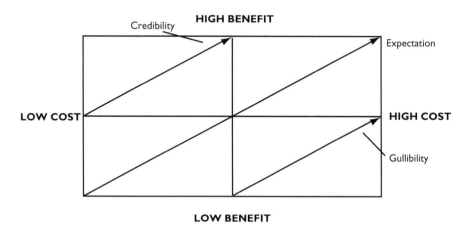

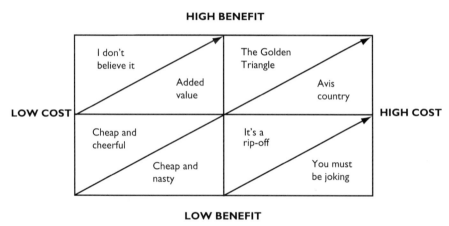

Figure 6.8 Baker's box

Exercise 6.1 The product demand curve

While the general relationship between price and quantity illustrated by the demand curve is true, with only very limited exceptions, for all products and markets, its practical application is fraught with difficulty. The main reason for this is that buyer behaviour is dynamic and that the firm's product represents only one of thousands of possible alternatives on which consumers could spend their disposable income. According to circumstances, the salience of the product and the consumers' felt need for it may vary widely and with it the price elasticity of demand which determines the actual inflection of the demand curve. As we shall see when we come to discuss pricing as an element of the marketing mix, there are some useful rules of thumb related to price elasticity but the point we are making here is that it is rarely possible to predict accurately how demand will react to price so allowing us to construct an accurate demand curve.

Despite this, managers should seek to project their feelings and expectations about the price–quantity relationship by constructing what they believe is the general shape of the demand curve for the generic product (floorcoverings, PCs, package holidays, diaries or whatever). Once you have done this you should identify which price bracket(s) your major competitors are serving and which you feel represent the best opportunity given your cost base. So, draw in your product's demand curve using the appropriate units.

Exercise 6.2 The product life cycle curve

Like the demand curve, the PLC curve's main value (in my opinion) lies in the insight it gives into the nature of competition associated with its various stages and the most appropriate tactics related to them. Because the PLC illustrates a generalized model of the substitution of new and improved products for older and less attractive alternatives it is unlikely that it will map over precisely the life history of any specific product or market. In other words, you can only use it for deduction, *not* prediction. Indeed the real value of the PLC is to remind us of the dangers of marketing myopia and, equally important, the potential for managerial intervention to take the greatest advantage of the various stages. In order to do this, however, it is necessary first to diagnose at what stage in its life cycle is the technology underlying the industry and then the stage of the life cycle in which our product is to be found. For example genetic engineering is in the embryonic phase (!) while micro-electronics is in the growth phase and paint products in the mature/decline phase.

I At what stage is the industry life cycle?

    Embryonic

    Growth

    Mature

    Decline

2 Draw the PLC for your product in the space below. Remember the key dimensions are output/sales over time.

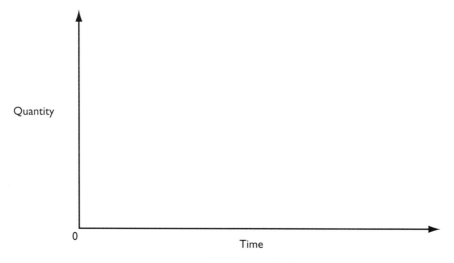

PLC for product

Exercise 6.3 Ansoff's growth/vector matrix

Ansoff's matrix is a simplified version of the technology market matrix developed by Johnson and Jones (1957). Both models underline the basic message implicit in the PLC – all products will die eventually, so you need to take deliberate steps to preserve and extend their life for as long as possible. At the same time you need to plan for succession and develop a portfolio of products at different stages of their life cycle. Plot the present (P) and future (F) position of each of your major products in the matrix provided, with an arrow indicating the direction of movement.

New market			
Extended market			
No change			
	No change	Improved technology	New technology

↑
Increasing
market
newness

Increasing technological newness →

Exercise 6.4 The directional policy matrix (DPM)

No doubt you will have recognized that the DPM developed by Shell is closely related to the SWOT analysis and provides a convenient way of summarizing where your products are in relation to the market opportunity. To complete the DPM for your firm you are required simply to exercise your judgement as to whether the end-use market is Attractive (embryonic/growth), Average (mature) or Unattractive (decline). Then for each market, how do you rate your own product's performance – Strong, Average or Weak? Write in the name of each product in the appropriate box and then use the generic strategy options to diagnose what needs to be done. A word of caution here. You may find some of your products (your only product?) is average or weak in an unattractive or average market. If so, you will need to devise a survival or exit strategy to enable you to capitalize your assets with a view to redeployment. Otherwise liquidation is the likely consequence.

		Market		
		Unattractive	Average	Attractive
	Weak			
Product	Average			
	Strong			

Exercise 6.5 The Boston box

The Boston box is essentially a matrix representation of the PLC curve. Its added value is that it requires the analyst to quantify growth rate and market share. While the latter measure is only really meaningful for major players at the industry level, e.g. Coca-Cola, Pepsi Cola, Schweppes, etc. in the carbonated beverages market, representing your own and competitors' shares using proportionately sized circles can give a vivid picture of the competitive position within the market.

If such an analysis is meaningful for you and you have the data, by all means complete your own Boston box.

Relative competitive position
(Market share)

	HIGH	LOW
HIGH		
LOW		

Annual market growth rate

Exercise 6.6 Baker's box

This box is simply an elaboration of the usual perceptual map represented by two dimensions at right angles to each other. By enclosing the dimensions in a rectangle and drawing in some diagonals it is possible to define the 'zone' within which competition can occur and suggest some labels to describe each of the positions. To complete your Baker's box, all you have to do is plot where your own and competitors' products are positioned.

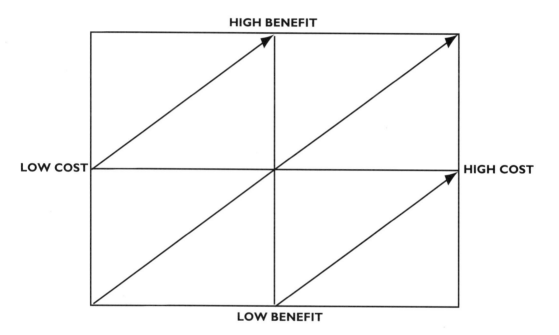

Now that we have identified some of the key strategic options open to any firm we need to select the one best suited to our own organization. To do so, we must first clarify the firm's mission.

Clarifying the firm's mission

In Chapter 19 of *Marketing, Strategy and Management* we deal with the development of a marketing culture at some length, and conclude that while the concept of a firm's mission is fairly clear, its definition is decidedly fuzzy. Klemm *et al.* (1989) found there was no single definition and their survey of *Times 1000* companies identified a variety of terms which embrace the concept:

- mission statement;
- corporate statement;
- aims and values;
- purpose;
- principles;
- objectives;
- goals;
- responsibilities and obligations.

Based on this analysis Klemm *et al.* detected a hierarchy in the use of these terms which they then define as follows:

Statement 1: The mission
A statement of the long-term purpose of the organization reflecting deeply held corporate views.

Statement 2: Strategic objectives
A statement of long-term strategic objectives outlining desired direction and performance in broad terms.

Statement 3: Quantified planning targets
Objectives in the form of quantified planning targets over a specific period.

Statement 4: The business of definition
A statement outlining the scope and activities of the company in terms of industry and geographical spread.

Put another way, the mission is an enduring quality which reflects cultural norms and values – it is the *raison d'être* of the organization. By contrast, 'vision' represents the current leader's interpretation of the achievement of the mission while 'strategy' is the means whereby specific action plans are measured against the benchmark of the vision to establish if this is being implemented in accordance with the objectives and targets.

Obviously the mission is highly specific to the organization and must be articulated by those currently responsible for its culture and values. Despite the difficulty of doing this without resorting to banal 'motherhoods' or generalizing to the point of becoming meaningless, it is vital that those responsible for strategic direction seek to capture this elusive quality and then ensure that their strategies and plans are congruent with it. If they don't, failure is likely because those responsible for implementation and delivery will be unable to buy into the strategy and plan.

If your organization has a mission statement such as Marks and Spencer or British Airways as reported in *Marketing Strategy and Management* – use it. If not, you will have to develop your own and then secure its endorsement in your own organization by the great majority of current employees.

Exercise 6.7 Mission statement

Write in your mission statement here.

Setting corporate objectives

Pre-eminent among managerial roles is the determination of courses of action which will realize the maximum potential of the resources – human, physical, financial and technological – which have been entrusted to their safekeeping. In order to achieve this managers must be able to identify the various possibilities open to them (hence the SWOT analysis) and then select that strategy or course of action which holds the greatest promise of success. In other words, one must set *objectives*.

However, in and of itself, setting objectives is a sterile and pointless exercise unless there is also a system for monitoring their achievement. It follows that vague and imprecise statements of the 'We intend to become the biggest/best/ most profitable or whatever company in our industry' kind are inadequate for this purpose. The science of gunnery is all about hitting targets but to do so you must first establish exactly where the target is in relation to your own position. That done, it is imperative to take into account all the factors which may influence the trajectory of the missile from the point of firing to the point of impact and make appropriate adjustments to compensate for them. Precision is everything. For example a very small deviation at the point of initiation can result in completely missing the target on the basis that $1°$ subtends a distance of 100 yards at a range of 6000 yards. It follows that if you are not pointing in the right direction to begin with it is highly unlikely that you will arrive at the intended destination. Thus objectives must satisfy at least three conditions:

1 They must define a precise end result.
2 They must set out the conditions and assumptions on which they are based.

3 They must spell out the performance indicators and timetable to be used in assessing their achievement.

For example a specific objective satisfying these conditions might be:

> In the financial year ending on 31 December 1999 we will increase our sales of widgets by ten per cent in the domestic market having increased prices by six per cent, to allow for the assumed rate of inflation for the period, and maintaining our marketing expenditure:sales ratio at twelve per cent.

In discussing marketing objectives Peter Drucker (1954) identifies seven which he believes must be given explicit consideration in any company:

1 The desired standing of the existing products in their market in turnover and percentage share measured against direct and indirect competition.
2 The desired standing of existing products in new markets measured as in point 1.
3 The existing products which should be phased out and ultimately abandoned, and the future product mix.
4 The new products needed in existing markets, the number, their properties and the share targets.
5 The new markets which new products will help to develop, in size and share.
6 The distribution organization needed to accomplish the marketing goals and the pricing policy appropriate to them.
7 A service objective, measuring how well customers should be supplied with what they consider value.

Implicit in this approach is the concept of a portfolio of products which may be at quite different stages in their life cycle, as spelled out in the analytical framework proposed by the Boston Consulting Group.

McKay (*Marketing Mystique*) identifies only three basic marketing objectives – to enlarge the market, to increase market share and to improve profitability – but then proceeds to spell out a number of distinct strategies for achieving these objectives:

1 To enlarge the market
  (a) By innovation or product development
    1 Through improving existing products or lines to increase use
    2 Through developing new products or lines
  (b) By innovation or market development
    1 Through developing present end-use markets
    2 Through discovering new end-use markets

2 To increase market share
  (a) By emphasizing product development and product improvement for competitive advantage
    1 Through product performance
    2 Through product quality
    3 Through product features
  (b) By emphasizing persuasion effort for competitive advantage
    1 Through sales and distribution
    2 Through advertising and sales promotion
  (c) By emphasizing customer-service activities for competitive advantage
    1 Through ready availability, order handling and delivery service
    2 Through credit and collection policies
    3 Through after-sales product service
3 To improve profitability
  (a) By emphasizing sales volume for profit leverage
    1 Through strengthened sales and distribution effort
    2 Through strengthened advertising and sales promotion effort
    3 Through strengthened advertising effort
  (b) By emphasizing elimination of unprofitable activities
    1 Through pruning products and lines
    2 Through pruning sales coverage and distribution
    3 Through pruning customer services
  (c) By emphasizing price improvement
    1 Through leadership in initiating needed price increases
    2 Through price improvement gained by differentiating products and services from those of competitors
  (d) By emphasizing cost reduction
    1 Through improved effectiveness of marketing tools and methods in product planning, in persuasion activities and in customer service activities.

McKay then proceeds to offer a series of guidelines for formulating objectives and strategies based upon his own extensive review of the literature. The majority of these have already been covered in the preceding discussion, but it is worth stressing the point made by McKay that: 'Each strategy carries with it certain essential related commitments, which must be accepted when the strategy is selected.'

In his book *The Strategic and Operational Planning of Marketing* (McGraw-Hill, 1986) Gordon Greenley provides a useful synthesis of the types of organizational objectives described in the marketing and strategic planning literature. This list, reproduced as Table 6.3, does not claim to be exhaustive nor does it follow that any particular organization will wish to develop measures for all those listed. However, as an *aide-mémoire* you should find it useful.

Table 6.3 Range of organizational objectives

Group 1: Directional objectives

Market leadership, measured by:

competitive position
degree of innovation
technological advances

Market spread, measured by:

number of markets
number of customer groups
number of industries
number of countries

Customer service, measured by:

product utility
product quality
product reliability

Group 2: Performance objectives

Growth, measured by:

sales revenue
volume output
profit margin
contribution

Profitability, measured by:

return on capital employed
return on assets
profit margin on sales revenue
return on shareholders' funds

Group 3: Internal objectives

Efficiency, measured by:

sales on total assets
stock turnover
credit period
liquidity
department costs on sales

Personnel, measured by:

employee relations and morale
personal development
average employee remuneration
sales revenue per employee

Group 4: External objectives

Social responsibility, measured by:

corporate image
price/profit relationship
resource utilization
public activity
community welfare

Exercise 6.8 Setting objectives

In the space below, list your major objectives:

Directional objectives

Performance objectives

Internal objectives

External objectives

Stating assumptions

In the previous exercises we have attempted to identify and collate as much information as we can, for the simple reason that if we have perfect information then, by definition, we are in a state of certainty and so do not have a problem. Problems exist because we have only partial information. It is for this reason that we have stressed the methodical collection of as much information as possible as an essential prerequisite to problem solving. However, in this task we are faced with three major difficulties – first, data are frequently incomplete, second, much information is presented in the form of opinion, and third, information may only be inferred from the apparent relationship between facts and events. It follows that a major job of the analyst is to screen all the available evidence for accuracy, validity and reliability as a preliminary to determining whether any relationships exist between acceptable facts that are suggestive of a solution to the problem in hand. There are many textbooks which deal with these issues at length and only a brief review is merited here.

As we noted in Chapter 2, while complete accuracy constitutes truth it would be erroneous to infer that less than complete accuracy is untruth and thereby unacceptable. In a business context it is rare that we require the degree of precision necessary in the scientific laboratory, or even the engineering workshop, and a reasonable estimate will often suffice. What is reasonable depends upon the circumstances and may vary by several percentage points around the true value, e.g. an estimate of market size. Essentially the need for accuracy depends upon how sensitive the final outcome of the analysis is to changes in the value of constituent elements – if the end result appears to be largely insensitive, then approximation will suffice; if highly sensitive, then the more accurate the point estimate the better.

A good example of this is provided by a feasibility study of the suitability of a Scottish mountain for development as a ski slope. While access to the slope, nature of the uplift facilities and back-up facilities (car parks, toilets, cafes, etc.), price to be charged, growth trends in total demand, etc. all have a bearing upon the decision, estimates of all these parameters are relatively unimportant compared with the value of the critical or limiting factor – the prevailing weather conditions. In the event, analysis revealed that when the number of days when it would not be possible to ski due to high winds or poor visibility were deducted from the total days on which snow could be guaranteed, the residue was so small as to make it quite obvious that a commercial venture was impractical almost regardless of the values attached to any of the other parameters.

The mark of a good analyst is an ability to isolate the critical factors and then focus all available resources in eliciting the most accurate information available concerning them. When using data from published sources the analyst must distinguish between the credibility to be attached to government statistics gathered by census and estimates extrapolated from samples by trade associations, consultants and those with a vested interest in the interpretation of the data they convey. The analyst must be conscious of recency and assess how a delay in publishing data may affect its current validity. The analyst must also be sensitive to changes in the collection and recording of data over time and satisfied as to the comparability of such data.

Such strictures are all very well when dealing with information from published sources, but how does one deal with opinion and hearsay? Much information in business problems falls into the latter category and is often conflicting in its indication of the true state of affairs. A classic example of this is to be found in many analyses when executive managers responsible for the finance, production and sales functions may each attribute the company's declining fortunes to a different cause, as they do in the Barnstaple Company case study. However, by carefully adducing factual data, or inferences which may be drawn from these data with a very high degree of confidence, it can be clearly demonstrated that usually only one manager's opinion is acceptable. Herein lies a key skill of the analyst – an ability to pick out relevant pieces of information, while discarding those which only serve to confuse an issue, and link them together to demonstrate a functional relationship.

It is possible to distinguish three different levels of analysis in this sorting and synthesizing process – deduction, inference and the formulation of assumptions. A deduction is made when one derives a logically necessary conclusion about a specific case from perfect information concerning the general case – for example all retailers of cars operate on a fifteen per cent gross margin; the XYZ company is a retailer of cars: *deduction* – the XYZ company operates on a fifteen per cent gross margin.

The status of an inference is less clear-cut than is that of a deduction. An inference may be defined as the interpretation placed upon evidence by an observer, from which it follows that the quality of an inference may range from excellent, i.e. a very high probability that it reflects reality, to very poor. Assuming, however, that the correct inference is drawn, then the distinction rests in the fact that there is always an element of uncertainty associated with an inference while there is none with a deduction. However, by linking logical deductions with reasonable inferences we can proceed a long way towards the solution of a problem.

The need for assumptions only arises where there is an absence of evidence necessary to link other information which seems to bear upon the problem. Assumptions may be of two kinds – working assumptions and critical assumptions. Working assumptions are those necessary to move an argument along and provide links in the chain of reasoning, but unlike critical assumptions they are not vital to the final decision. In every case an assumption should only be made as a last resort, when it is obvious that other information is not available. When setting out an assumption, and especially a critical assumption, it is important to state clearly the evidence considered in deriving the assumption, the reasons for selecting and rejecting particular points, and the precise form of the final assumption made. Only by careful attention to these factors will analysts be able to communicate the thought processes leading to their conclusion; without them their argument will be open to criticism and lack conviction.

From the foregoing it is obvious that *both* the drawing of inferences and the formulation of assumptions demand the exercise of judgement, and this is the proper role for its application. In all other cases a strictly formal and factual approach should be followed.

Bearing these comments in mind, and in light of the conclusions drawn from your situation analysis, you should now set down those issues which have an important bearing upon the achievement of your objectives but about which you have incomplete and/or imperfect information. In the case of each factor you must then state your own working assumption as the basis of developing the action plan to move you from where you are to where you want to be, e.g.

Issue/Factor   The rate of inflation for the next one, three, five years.

Assumption   It is assumed inflation will increase to six per cent next year but will then settle down at four per cent per annum for the next four years.

Exercise 6.9 Stating assumptions

Write down your own list of critical issues/factors based on your marketing appreciation and your assumptions concerning them.

Issue/Factor

Assumption

Issue/Factor

Assumption

Issue/Factor

Assumption

Issue/Factor

Assumption

Issue/Factor

Assumption

Issue/Factor

Assumption

Issue/Factor

Assumption

Issue/Factor

Assumption

Issue/Factor

Assumption

Issue/Factor

Assumption

Selecting a core strategy

According to Michael Porter (1990): 'There are two basic types of competitive advantage: *lower cost* and *differentiation*'.

As we noted earlier, lower cost is usually associated with economies of scope and scale, especially in the marketing function (promotion, selling and distribution). Thus lower cost is a strategy only available to large organizations. In most countries ninety per cent or more of people work for firms with fewer than 200 employees. For them differentiation is the only viable source of competitive advantage.

In *Competitive Strategy* (1980) Porter identifies three generic strategies which he labels *cost leadership, differentiation* and *focus,* and distinguishes between differentiation and focus in suggesting that the former is appropriate to large firms which have a large portfolio of complementary products catering for the needs of different segments of the same market. By contrast, focus applies to small firms with a limited range of products serving small niche markets.

Table 6.4 Alternative strategies

Strategy	Characteristics
Undifferentiated	● Firm has one marketing mix for the entire market. ● This strategy rests on the assumption of user homogeneity and/or an implicit acceptance that there is no prior ability to segment a market and so must appeal to all of it. ● Firms follow this strategy on the precept that what's good for the market is good for them. ● Such a strategy is rarely successful because markets are not homogeneous but are made up of different types of buyers with diverse wants regarding product benefits, price, channels of distribution and service.
Differentiated	● This is the policy of attacking the market by tailoring separate product and marketing programmes for each segment. ● This strategy implies an ability to segment a market and to cater for the varying needs of the different segments. ● Firms will tend to concentrate their efforts on selected segments which they will seek to dominate. ● Firms will have several marketing mixes.
Concentrated (focus)	● Activities are concentrated on a particular market with a view to achieving a stronger position within that market, e.g. through further investment and/or aggressive marketing. ● Firms will have one marketing mix. ● This is often the best strategy for the smaller firm.

While Porter used new labels for his generic strategies the concept had been familiar to marketers for some time in their classification of alternative strategies as *undifferentiated, differentiated* and *concentrated*. The characteristics of these strategies are summarized in Table 6.4.

Exercise 6.10 Selecting a core strategy

Based on the above definitions, you should now select your core strategy and write in a short statement justifying your selection.

We intend to follow a strategy of _____ because:

Having decided on your core strategy, the next decision is the *approach* you intend to follow. Again, in very simple terms there are only two alternatives – *push* and *pull*. The characteristics of these may be summarized as shown in Table 6.5.

Table 6.5 Alternative approaches

Approaches	Characteristics
Push	● With this approach the firm 'markets' the product/service only to the next person in the distribution chain, i.e. the products are 'pushed' down to the end-user ● Greater emphasis on personal selling
Pull	● With this approach the firm concentrates activities on 'marketing' to the end-user with a view to creating strong demand for the product/service. This demand will 'pull' the product down through the distribution chain ● Emphasis on advertising and promotion

Exercise 6.11 Core strategy and approach

Now you have selected your core strategy and approach, summarize these for each of your products on the following pro forma.

Product group	Alternatives			Approach	
	Undifferentiated	Differentiated	Concentrated	Push	Pull

To conclude this chapter we look finally at the techniques of segmentation and positioning as a basis for selecting the specific markets in which we intend to compete.

Segmentation, targeting and positioning

In our earlier discussion of customer analysis (Chapter 5) we deferred detailed consideration on the grounds that until we have clear objectives on which markets to serve and what products/services to supply, a great deal of time and effort could be wasted on gathering irrelevant data. Now that we have a clearer view of where we want to go it is time to define precisely who our intended customers are and how we propose to reach them. In other words – segmentation, targeting and positioning.

In economics the analysis of supply and demand is greatly simplified by the assumption that products and consumers are homogeneous. By contrast, psychology starts from the assumption that every individual differs from every other in some respect – a concept of total heterogeneity. While there are markets in which the products may be considered homogeneous for all practical purposes, e.g. commodities, materials, etc., few would make the mistake of assuming that all buyers will behave in the same way. Similarly, there are markets, particularly for services, where every customer will be treated as an individual. But, in the great majority of cases, a compromise will have to be struck between homogeneity and heterogeneity and it is here that the concept of segmentation comes into play. In essence, the concept of market segmentation rests upon recognition of a differentiated demand for a product while its use as a marketing tool depends upon identification of the most appropriate variables with which to subdivide total demand into economically viable submarkets or *segments*. By 'economically viable' we mean of sufficient size and potential profitability to make it worth the sellers' while to cater to the specific needs of members of that segment.

Before looking at some of the more popular approaches to segmentation it will be worth while reminding ourselves about the distinction between *market segmentation* and *product differentiation* as alternative marketing strategies.

In the first flush of enthusiasm for the 'new' marketing many people dismissed product differentiation as reflecting a production orientation in that it depended on the producers' view of what the market wanted. By contrast, market segmentation is based on the principle that we determine what the customer needs and then set about creating a supply of that product – a marketing orientation. The only problem with total acceptance of this view is that customers don't always know what they want, so there is no practical way of establishing this in advance of committing ourselves to producing a product.

As a generalization, the more familiar the generic product and the more mature the market, the more likely it is that we will be able to practise market segmentation. By contrast, the more innovative the product the less possible it becomes to pre-identify specific submarkets. Only by selling the product will it become apparent what kinds of customers are particularly attracted to it. While we may make assumptions about the likely customers we will not be able to profile them or define segments until we have actual experience of buyer behaviour. It follows that in developing radically new products or on entering unfamiliar new markets we will have to depend upon our judgement and perception of a market opportunity in targeting those customers for whom it is felt the new product will have the greatest appeal.

Where there is an established market, then it is possible to profile customers and diagnose distinct segments following a multistep process as shown in Figure 6.9.

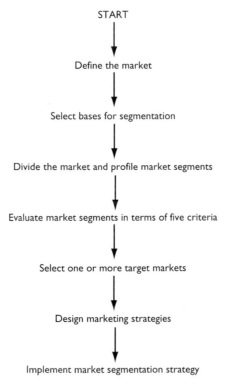

Figure 6.9 The multistep market segmentation process

For the purposes of this model a *market segment* may be defined as:

> A group of individuals, groups or organizations that share one or more similar characteristics which make them have relatively similar product needs.

The five criteria are that a segment should be:

- measurable;
- accessible;
- substantial;
- unique in its response;
- stable in its behaviour.

Finally, a *target market* is:

> A group of persons or organizations for whom a firm creates and maintains a marketing mix that is designed to meet the specific needs and preferences of that group.

In sum, market segmentation allows a company to:

- view a market from the customer's point of view;
- exploit its strengths better by selecting compatible market segments;
- develop more sharply focused strategies aimed at market requirements;
- identify gaps in the market which offer new product opportunities.

There is a large number of variables which can be used separately or in combination to segment a market. In *Marketing* (1996) we summarize these as shown in Table 6.6.

Table 6.6 Major segmentation variables

Demographics	age, sex, education, occupation, income, social class, family/household status, life-cycle stage, religion, nationality, race
Location/geography	type of property, urban, suburban, rural, region, country, climatic zone
Geodemographic	combination of demography and geography
Psychographic	personality, perception, motivation
Lifestyle	AIO (attitudes, interests, opinions)
Behavioural	benefits sought, usage, loyalty preference, perceptions, readiness stage (unaware, aware, informed, interested, desirous, intending to buy), marketing factor sensitivity (quality, price, service, advertising, sales promotion, etc.)
Organizational	composition of DMU (decision-making unit) – household, organization, loyalty, reciprocity, etc.

The factors listed in Table 6.6 are mainly applicable to consumer markets. For organizational markets, the factors shown in Tables 6.7 and 6.8 of macro and micro bases for segmentation may be more appropriate.

Table 6.7 Key micro bases of segmentation

Variables	Illustrative breakdown
Key criteria	quality, delivery, supplier, reputation
Decision-specific conflict	high … low
Purchasing strategies	optimizer, satisficer
Structure of decision-making unit	major decision participants, e.g. purchasing manager and plant manager
Importance of purchase	high importance … low importance
Attitude towards vendors	favourable … unfavourable
Organizational innovativeness	innovator … follower
Personal characteristics	
Demographics	age, educational background
Decision style	normative, conservative, mixed mode
Risk	risk taker, risk avoider
Confidence	high confidence, low confidence
Job responsibility	purchasing, production, engineering

Source: Hutt, M.D. and Speh, T.W. (1995). *Business Marketing Management*. Dryden Press.

Table 6.8 Key macro bases of segmentation

Variables	Illustrative breakdowns
Characteristics of buying organizations	
Size (the scale of operations of the organization)	small, medium, large – based on sales or number of employees
Geographical location	Germany, France, Italy, UK, Norway
Usage rates	non-user, light user, moderate user, heavy user
Structure of procurement	centralized, decentralized
Product application	
SIC category	varies by product
End-market served	varies by product
Characteristics of purchasing situation	
Type of buying situation	new buy, modified rebuy, straight rebuy
Stage in purchase decision process	early stages, late stages

Source: Hutt, M.D. and Speh, T.W. (1995). *Business Marketing Management*. Dryden Press.

In addition to the different factors available for segmenting business and consumer markets, we should also bear in mind that:

- small numbers might lead to non-viable segments;
- large customers with unique needs might constitute a 'segment' in their own right;
- consumer motivations may be difficult to identify; business motivations are more obvious;
- consumer markets, *appear* to be characterized by their homogeneity;
- business markets *appear* to be characterized by their heterogeneity.

As the above summary of some of the key considerations to be taken into account in segmenting a market makes clear, the selection of appropriate factors or criteria depends very much on the specific context. To provide some practice in developing your own factor rating table we have chosen a decision with which everyone is familiar – taking a holiday. Further, we have chosen to isolate the basic drivers of behaviour – *motivation* and *benefits sought*.

The structure of Exercises 6.12 and 6.13 will be familiar to you. Based on a review of the available research we have created two rating tables, one covering motives, the other benefits sought. You should complete stage 1 by rank ordering the factors in order of importance to you personally. Then, if you are working with a group, hold a meeting and see how well you can reconcile the different interests by clustering individuals into subgroups and defining them as a segment.

The experts' rankings for stage 3 are to be found at page 218 in Appendix A and should be entered into column 3 so that you can complete stages 4 and 5. When it comes to interpreting your choice of factors by comparison with the experts, the important thing to remember is that the experts' ranking is a generalized statement so that a product conforming to their rankings would appeal to the 'average' holidaymaker. The whole point about segmentation is to see if you can specify differentiated products which satisfy the five criteria referred to earlier.

Sources

The first set of factors is a list of the main reasons, or motivation, why individuals chose to go on holiday. This list, and the expert ranking that relates to it, comes from a study by J. Krippendorf (1987).

The second of these two exercises presents a list of the benefits sought by holidaymakers in their choice of destination. This list, and the expert answers that relate to the exercise, come from two sources. First, a study by the Carinthia Tourist Board (Austria) which looked at the most frequently selected criteria when evaluating Austrian holiday destinations. This study is described in the *Tourism Marketing and Management Handbook* edited by S. F. Witt and L. Moutinho (1994). The second study is described by R. Teare *et al.*'s *Marketing in Hospitality and Tourism* (1994) and relates to Alpine holiday destinations. This study again examined the importance of benefits to holidaymakers in their choice of destination and ranked these in order of importance.

To produce the experts' ranking these two studies were considered. The rankings for the two studies were correlated to produce an answer that 'averaged' the rankings for both studies. Place-specific factors that directly related to the original studies were ignored, e.g. museum opening hours, mountaineering and nudist bathing.

The main motives for travel and tourism

Listed below are the different types of motives that people have for going on holiday and travelling. The list comes from *Marketing in Travel and Tourism* by V. T. C. Middleton (1994). It uses contributions from Valerie Smith (1977), Murphy (1985) and McIntosh and Goeldner (1990) and according to Middleton is compatible with the classification of travel purposes developed by the World Tourism Organization. As you can see, this classification is more general than the factors listed in the exercises.

Business/work-related motives
Pursuit of private and public sector business, conferences, meetings, short courses.
Travel away from home for work-related purposes, including airline personnel, truck drivers, service engineers.

Physical/physiological motives
Participation in indoor sport and active outdoor recreation such as golfing, walking, sailing, skiing.
Undertaking activities in pursuit of health, fitness, recuperation.
Resting/relaxing/generally unwinding from stress of everyday life.
Finding warmth/sunshine/relaxation on a beach.

Cultural/psychological/personal/education motives
Participation in festivals, theatre, music, museums – as spectator, player or volunteer.
Participation in personal interests, including intellectual, craft and other leisure-time pursuits.
Visiting destinations for the sake of their cultural and/or natural heritage (including ecotourism).

Social/interpersonal and ethnic motives
Enjoying the company of friends and relatives.
Undertaking social duty occasions – from weddings to funerals.
Accompanying others travelling for other reasons, such as business or social duty.
Visiting the place of one's birth.

Entertainment/amusement/pleasure/pastime motives
Watching sport/other spectator events.
Visiting theme parks/amusement parks.
Undertaking leisure shopping.

Religious motives
Participating in pilgrimages.
Undertaking retreats for meditation and study.

Exercise 6.12 Motives for going on holiday

Motive for holiday	Stage 1 – Individual ranking	Stage 2 – Team ranking	Stage 3 – Experts' ranking	Stage 4 – Difference between stages 1 and 3	Stage 5 – Difference between stages 2 and 3
a Eat well					
b Recover strength					
c Experience other countries					
d Get exercise, sports and games activities					
e Be with other people, have company					
f Experience a great deal, have diversity					
g Switch off, relax					
h Get away from everyday life					
i Experience something entirely different					
j Do as one pleases, be free					
k Cleaner air, cleaner water, get out of the polluted environment					
l Have time for one another					
m Get sunshine, escape bad weather					
n Have a lot of fun and entertainment					
o Experience nature					
				Total:	Total:

Exercise 6.13 Benefits sought when choosing holiday destinations

Benefit sought	Stage 1 – Individual ranking	Stage 2 – Team ranking	Stage 3 – Experts' ranking	Stage 4 – Difference between stages 1 and 3	Stage 5 – Difference between stages 2 and 3
a Festivals/folklore					
b Uncrowded/ peaceful					
c Family orientation					
d Unspoilt/ attractive environment					
e Fitness facilities					
f Value for money					
g Climate/weather					
h Picturesque-ness					
i Children's arrangements					
j Shopping facilities					
k Good restaurants					
l Good eating and drinking facilities					
m Friendly service					
n Sightseeing/ cultural life/ excursions					
o Recreational facilities					
p Entertainment facilities					
q Accommodation					
r Friendliness of locals					
s Accessibility					
				Total:	Total:

Once you have completed these exercises you should create your own rating table by entering your criteria for your product/market into the blank pro forma provided – Exercise 6.14.

Exercise 6.14 Segmentation performance appraisal

Product:

Segmentation factor	Weighting	Performance						Score
		1	2	3	4	5	N/A	

Product:

Segmentation factor	Weighting	Performance						Score
		1	2	3	4	5	N/A	

Product:

Segmentation factor	Weighting	Performance						Score
		1	2	3	4	5	N/A	

Targeting and positioning

The objective of segmentation is to *disaggregate* the total market into viable submarkets. The objective of targeting and positioning is to decide which of the segments you are going to compete in and how you intend to differentiate (position) yourself from other firms serving the same segment.

  To implement a policy of target marketing the following procedure should be followed:

Implementing a policy of target marketing

Identification
Which specific variables should be used?
Which descriptor variables should be used?

Assessment
What are the important criteria for evaluating the segments?
Which of the segments are actionable?
Which of the resulting segments are the most desirable?

Differentiation
Position the product for the target segment(s)
Assemble a marketing mix for the target segment(s).

Which specific variables should be used?

Included among the objective, or more objective, of these variables would be:

Product usage/purchase rates
Are they non-users, medium users, heavy users?
Are they solus users, in that they only buy one brand?
Are they purchasers of interest as well as the users?

User/buyer status
Are they current users, former users, non-users, potential users, regular users, first-time users? Again, in some cases, it may be the buyers who are of interest rather than the users.

Loyalty status
What degree of brand loyalty do they display? Is it strong, medium, or weak?

Marketing factor sensitivity
How do they respond to the various marketing influences? Are they susceptible to price or to advertising?

Purchasing situation and occasion
Is it impulse or considered purchase?
Is the context social or business?
What is the setting for the purchase?

Media habits
What media are they exposed to?

From these variables, the target audience might be heavy users, with marked brand loyalty, who are price-sensitive. As for the more inferred measures, these might include:

Needs
What do they need, or say they need, from the product?

Benefits sought
What particular benefits do they expect from the product?

Attitudes and perceptions
What attitudes do they have towards the product? How is it perceived?

Product preferences
What do they prefer and how do they choose between brands?

Once you have defined and selected the chosen segment(s), the next step is to create a perceptual map of the segment and then plot how competitors compare in terms of the chosen dimensions. The principles underlying perceptual mapping were discussed earlier in the chapter. Perhaps the main point to re-emphasize here is that any of the six positions lying between the zones of credibility and gullibility may represent a viable market segment, although some are clearly to be preferred over others.

Using the pro forma provided in Exercise 6.15 you should now develop a perceptual map for each segment in which you intend to compete, indicating clearly the position occupied by your competitors and where it is you intend to position yourself (see Figure 6.10).

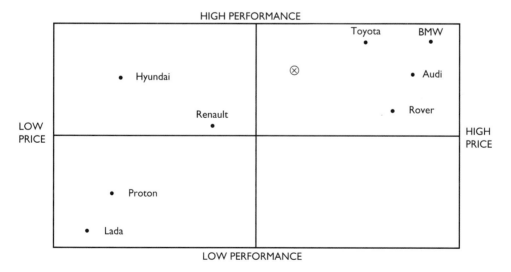

Perceptual plot for mid-range saloon cars (hypothetical!)

⊗ Chosen position

Figure 6.10 Example of a perceptual map

Exercise 6.15 Positioning maps

Now complete your own positioning maps for each of your products.

Chapter 7

How do I get there?

Introduction

In the preceding chapter we undertook a series of exercises to enable us to answer the question: 'Where do I want to go?'. Now that we have established our core strategy and chosen market segment(s), the next step is to develop operational marketing plans to implement the chosen strategy and answer the question: 'How do I get there?'.

The chapter contains three main parts. To begin with, we look at the idea of a marketing mix comprising four main elements around which a marketing plan may be constructed – product, price, place (or distribution) and promotion (4Ps). Having reviewed the broad policies associated with each of these core elements, we then examine each of the 4Ps in more detail with a view to issues of tactical application. Finally, the chapter looks at how the policies and tactics may be synthesized and integrated into a single, operational marketing plan.

The marketing mix

In *The Marketing Book* (Baker, 1994) Doyle observes:

> There are two key distinctions which are central to marketing management: the selection of target markets which determine where the firm will compete and the design of the marketing mix (product, price, promotion and distribution method) which will determine its success in these markets.

The marketing mix refers to the apportionment of effort, the combination, the designing, and the integration of the elements of marketing into a programme or 'mix' which, on the basis of an appraisal of the market forces, will best achieve the objectives of an enterprise at a given time. There is a wide diversity among marketers on which elements compose the marketing mix and there is no widely accepted list that can be used. Some of them talk of the marketing mix in terms of the 4Ps, i.e. product, price, place and promotion. Some others add a fifth element, i.e. after-sales service, while some marketers talk about seven Ps and one A – product, price, promotion, packaging, personal selling, publicity, physical distribution and advertising. In fact, the mix elements and their relative importance may differ from industry to industry, from company to company and quite often during the life of the product itself. Furthermore, the marketing mix must take full cognizance of the major *environmental dimensions* that prevail in the marketplace. This latter point adds a dynamic flavour to the marketing mix in so far as it has to be changed from time to time in response to new factors in the marketing scene.

In tailoring its mix a firm will seek to offer one which target customers will see as superior to that offered by competition. This goal of offering a marketing mix superior to competition is termed the *differential* advantage.

For the purposes of this book we will consider the marketing mix in terms of the 4Ps, which may be elaborated into a checklist as shown in Table 7.1.

Table 7.1 Components of the marketing mix

Product	Price	Promotion	Place
Quality	List price	Advertising	Distributors
Features	Discounts	Personal selling	Retailers
Name	Allowances	Sales promotion	Locations
Packaging	Credit	Direct marketing	Inventory
Services		Public relations	Transport
Guarantee			

As Table 7.1 shows, each of the 4Ps embraces a large number of factors each of which may be disaggregated still further. Given that the book is concerned with *strategic* marketing planning, we do not intend to examine these in the kind of detail which might be necessary in developing a fully operational marketing plan. There are several books which have been developed for this purpose[1] that contain very detailed pro formas covering

[1] One of the best places to start a more detailed analysis is with:
Wilson, A. (1993). *Marketing Audit Checklists,* 2nd edition. McGraw-Hill.
Other useful references are:
Makens, James C. (1989). *The 12-day Marketing Plan.* Prentice Hall.
Hiebing Jnr, Roman G. and Cooper, Scott (1997). *The Successful Marketing Plan,* 2nd edition. NTC Books.
Cohen, William A. (1995). *The Marketing Plan.* Wiley.
Quain, William and Jarboe, Glen R. (1993). *The Marketing Plan Project Manual.* West Publishing Co.

every aspect of the marketing mix. If you are developing such a detailed marketing plan, then you should refer to one or more of these books for additional ideas once you have addressed the major issues discussed here.

Product policy

The primary concern of most organizations is product policy and management rather than market policy and management. Once a firm has committed itself to a given market all else flows from it and the decision is difficult if not impossible to reverse. As has been pointed out, choice of market:

> builds a set of relationships with customers that are at once a major
> source of strength and a major commitment. The commitment
> carries with it the responsibility to serve customers well, to stay in
> the technical and product development race, and to grow in pace
> with growing market demand.

In completing earlier exercises you will already have analysed many of the factors which have a critical bearing on product policy. For example in Exercise 4.1 you were asked to rank order sixteen factors identified as having an impact on a product's competitiveness. In executing the marketing appreciation (Chapter 5) the role of the product was central to several of the analyses and particularly the customer analysis (Exercise 5.6). Similarly, selecting a core strategy product performance and stage in the product life cycle were seen to be critical factors. Now is the time to synthesize and integrate these earlier analyses.

First, however, we need to summarize the current status of our product portfolio and we have developed a number of pro formas to help you do this. In Exercise 7.1 you are invited to summarize product sales by product, geographical area and market segment. If some other criteria seem more useful, then use these. Next we summarize product uses and then complete a review of substitute products to remind us where the immediate competition is coming from.

Exercise 7.1 Current status

Product sales

By product

Product/ service	Sales				
	19–	19–	19–	19–	19–

By geographical area

Product/service

Area	Sales				
	19–	19–	19–	19–	19–

By market segment

Product/service

Area	Sales				
	19–	19–	19–	19–	19–

Product uses

Product/ service	Major uses	Target market (for major uses)	Subsidiary uses	Target market (for subsidiary uses)
1				
2				
3				
4				

● Do existing customers know our full range and the major and subsidiary uses for the products/services?

Substitute products

Product/service
(Fill in a form for each product/service in your portfolio)

Substitute product(s)	Producing company	Similarities	Differences	Advantages	Disadvantages
		(of substitute product compared to your product)			

Now that we have summarized the current status it will be useful to compare this with our earlier customer analysis (Exercise 5.5) and complete an additional analysis as in Exercise 7.2.

There will be clear benefits if you can spell out some of the basic dimensions of user needs and this will make it that much easier to develop the appropriate product characteristics.

A very helpful approach to this process is to be found in a monograph published by the Design Council by Rothwell, Gardiner and Schott (1983) which provides a framework for this section. Rothwell *et al.* argue that user needs can be thought of as having four dimensions, which they define as follows:

- **Need elements** An indication of the overall price and specific performance characteristics required by customers.
- **Need intensity** A measure of the degree of importance given to each need element by potential users.
- **Need stability** A measure of the degree to which the need remains unchanged over time.
- **Need diffusion** A measure of how widely felt the need is. This defines the size of the potential market.

Using the product characteristics in Table 7.2 as a checklist, complete Exercise 7.2 for each target market.

Once Exercise 7.2 has been completed, you will have a simple bar chart which illustrates how need elements and need intensity can be combined to give a quick visualization of product configuration desired by each target market segment (see Figure 7.1).

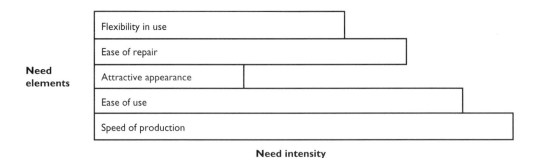

Figure 7.1 Bar chart showing need elements and need intensity

Table 7.2 Checklist of product characteristics

Technical	Economic	
	Non-price	*Price*
Size	Servicing costs	List price
Shape	Availability of parts and	Sale price
Weight	service	Net price after trade-in
Consistency	Running costs	allowance
Materials used in	Breakdown costs	Financing or leasing
construction	Depreciation	arrangements
Complexity	User training facilities	Discounts
Power source	Instructions	Sale or return
Power output	Delivery	Special offers
Speed/production rate		
Reliability		
Flexibility		
Ease of use		
Safety		
Appearance/design		
features		
Smell		
Taste		

Exercise 7.2 User needs

Product/service

Target market

Column 1 Need element	Column 2 Need intensity	Column 3 Need stability	Column 4 Need diffusion

- Using Table 7.2, list the appropriate need elements of the target market in column 1.
- In column 2, rate the need intensity of each element on a 5-point scale where 1 = important and 5 = unimportant.
- In column 3, rate the stability of each element on a 5-point scale where 1 = stable and 5 = unstable.
- In column 4, note the need diffusion of the need, i.e. how widely felt this need is within the target market.
- Create a bar chart of the need elements and their intensity (see Figure 7.1) in the space below.

These pictograms should be constructed for each market segment and, when combined with an evaluation of the need stability and need diffusion, they will enable you to decide which offer the best opportunities in terms of your firm's aspirations and supply capabilities.

Now that we have visualized the product configuration desired by each market segment we serve, it remains to relate this information to our earlier diagnosis of the PLC and product portfolio (page 115 ff) and the guidelines for product competitiveness from Exercise 4.1. To do this, complete Exercise 7.3.

Exercise 7.3 Product policy indications

At what stage of the PLC is the product? (introduction/growth/maturity/decline)	
What is the elasticity of demand? (elastic/unitary/inelastic)	
What is the current generic strategy? (undifferentiated/differentiated/ concentrated)	
What is your basic marketing approach? (push or pull)	
Which of Ansoff's strategies are you following? (penetration, product development, market development, diversification)	
Are your sales growing/stable/declining?	
Are there any close substitutes for your product?	
How well does your product meet user needs? (excellent/good/fair/poor)	

The purpose of this checklist is to pull together the conclusions from your earlier analysis into a single summary statement. With the exception of the generic strategy and basic marketing approach we have suggested a score for each answer with a possible maximum of 29 (see Appendix A). Obviously, the higher your score the greater the competitive advantage you enjoy; the lower the score the greater the competitive threat. As to strategy and approach, the higher your score the more freedom you have in choosing what you want to do bearing in mind your own size and resources *vis-à-vis* other members of the value chain, e.g. if you're small a concentrated strategy would be chosen.

With regard to the options suggested by Ansoff's growth/vector matrix we have suggested you score 1 for each, as research indicates that more successful firms pursue multiple strategies *simultaneously* (Baker and Hart, 1989).

Irrespective of how well you are doing in terms of your current product policy two further considerations must be borne in mind:

1 Change is inevitable – how robust is your new product development programme?
2 The 'product' is a combination of both physical attributes and related services.

The implication of the diagnostics discussed in Chapter 6 is clear – exchange is the outcome of the interaction between demand and supply, of markets and technologies, of customers and products. The objective of marketing is to try and anticipate changing customer needs and create products to satisfy them. In other words, new product development (NPD) must be an integral part of marketing strategy and strategic marketing planning. To help assess your NPD policies and performance, complete the following checklist (Exercise 7.4).

Exercise 7.4 NPD policies and performance

1 What percentage of your current sales is derived from products introduced:
   in the past year   _____%
   in the past five years   _____%

2 What percentage of your future sales will come from new products:
   next year   _____%
   next five years   _____%

3 Do you have a formal policy for NPD?
                               _____YES
                               _____NO

4 Which of the following approaches to NPD do you use? (Tick all that apply):
   New product committee   ☐
   Venture team   ☐
   New product department   ☐
   Product managers   ☐

5 Where do your ideas for new products come from?
   Customers   ☐
   Suppliers   ☐
   R&D   ☐
   Production   ☐
   Marketing   ☐
   Other   ☐

Interpretation of the checklist against the available evidence would suggest:

1 Successful firms derive a significant proportion of both sales and profits from new products and expect the trend to accelerate in future.
2 Successful firms have clearly articulated policies and objectives for NPD.
3 There is no single best way to organize for NPD but certain factors are more important than others (see Exercise 5.4 on critical success factors).
4 Successful firms source ideas as widely as possible.

The second dimension to be reviewed is service policy. In an increasingly competitive environment it seems reasonable to assume that as the potential for product differentiation is eroded one should give added consideration to the provision of services which will enhance both the physical performance of products and their perceived value in the customer's eyes. Even more important, through the provision of support services the supplier has the opportunity to increase the strength of the bond with existing customers and so reduce the risk of their 'switching' to alternative suppliers.

There is a working generalization that the more complex the product, the longer its working life and the greater the financial outlay upon it, the greater the need for customer service. Your analysis of user needs (Exercise 7.2) should also have given some indication of customer requirements with regard to service for your firm.

A useful approach classifies the elements of the service function into pre-transaction elements, transaction elements and post-transaction elements and these are described in Table 7.3.

Table 7.3 Classification of the elements of the service function

Pre-transaction	Relates to the corporate policies or programmes, e.g. written statements of service policy, adequacy of organizational structure and system flexibility.
Transaction	Customer service variables directly involved in performing the physical distribution function, e.g. product availability, order cycle time (average and consistency), order status information, order preparation, order size and order frequency.
Post-transaction	These are generally supportive of the product while in use, e.g. product warranty, parts and repair service, procedures for customer complaints and product replacements.

Exercise 7.5 Current service offerings

In order to evaluate possible changes in service strategy it will be necessary to undertake research among your customers and compare the results with the existing provision. Exercise 7.2 may have already gone some way towards doing this.

List the current service offerings for each product.

Product/service:

Target market:

	Current service
Pre-transaction	
Transaction	
Post-transaction	

● Comparing this with the results from Exercise 7.2, do you think there are any areas where the current service provision is deficient?

Price policy

In *Marketing Strategy and Management* (1992) we summarize some of the key issues to be considered as follows.

Like all other elements of the marketing mix, price should serve and help attain the firm's objectives. In the short run price has a direct and immediate influence on the firm's short-run profitability through its effect on sales volume, which in turn affects sales revenue and possibly unit cost of production and marketing as well. Further, in the medium to long run there is an indirect connection between prices and the firm's objectives, as prices affect the firm's cash flow, its inventories, its customers' inventories, its brand image, its quality image, the competitiveness of its markets, the likelihood of government regulation and customer awareness of, and concern with, price.

It is important to distinguish between the short and long run, particularly as we have already argued that short-run objectives may sometimes contradict long-run objectives. For example maximizing long-run profits may be achieved by restraining profits in the short run with a lower price, a higher product quality, or a more extensive promotional campaign than the one that would maximize short-run profits. Because of the inevitable uncertainty which surrounds the future there is a tendency for most pricing methods to concentrate on the short rather than the long run. Thus, Lawrence Fisher offers the following list of short-run pricing objectives:

1 To penetrate and pre-empt the market for a product by charging a low price.
2 To cream the market and obtain early profits and liquidity by charging a high price.
3 To assist in phasing out an obsolescent product by making it unattractively expensive.
4 To discourage competition from entering the market.
5 To avoid customer and political criticism.
6 To support a company image.
7 To encourage market expansion by a low-price/high-volume policy.
8 To avoid unduly provocative action which could lead to prices falling to a level inconsistent with long-term profitability.

Clearly, while these are proposed as short-run objectives, only one of them, point 3, is intrinsically incompatible with a long-run pricing objective, and even this may be seen as such in an indirect way, in that disposing of an obsolescent product enables resources to be diverted to new and potentially more profitable ends.

In *Marketing: Theory and Practice* (Baker, 1995) Diamontopolous suggests a taxonomy of pricing objectives as shown in Table 7.4.

From this and his survey of pricing in practice Diamontopolous identifies three basic pricing methods as cost, demand and competition-orientated and summarizes the different approaches as shown in Table 7.5.

Table 7.4 Pricing objectives

Pricing objectives		
Profit ● Money profit ● Gross/net margin ● Contribution margin ● Return on sales ● Return on costs ● Return on capital employed ● Return on net worth ● Profit growth	**Volume** ● Market share ● Sales volume ● Sales revenue ● Sales growth ● Capacity utilization	**Financial** ● Cash flow ● Earnings per share ● Price earnings ratio ● Dividends
Competition orientated ● Matching/undercutting competition ● Avoidance of price wars ● Limit entry ● Price stability ● Money profit	**Customer orientated** ● Fair price levels ● Goodwill ● Value for money ● Full price range ● Price maintenance in the channel	**Miscellaneous** ● Projection of high quality image ● Avoidance of government intervention ● Survival/security

Table 7.5 Pricing methods

Pricing methods		
Cost orientated ● Cost-plus pricing ● Contribution pricing ● Target (ROI) pricing ● Price-minus pricing ● Return on costs	**Demand orientated** ● Marginal analysis ● Trial and error pricing ● Intuitive pricing ● Market pricing ● Monopsonistic pricing	**Competition orientated** ● Product analysis pricing ● Value pricing ● Price leadership/ followership ● Competitive parity pricing

Price plays an important role in the marketing mix for many reasons. In *Marketing* (1996) we cite six reasons proposed by Simon (1989) as follows:

1 Price elasticity is twenty times greater than advertising elasticity; that is, a one per cent change has a sales effect twenty times as big as a one per cent change in advertising expenditure.
2 The sales effect of a price change is often immediate, and so measurable, while changes in other mix variables are usually lagged and difficult to quantify.
3 Price changes are easy to effect compared with varying other mix variables.
4 Competitors react more quickly to price changes.

5 Price does not require an initially negative cash flow as do other marketing expenditures such as advertising which have a lagged effect.
6 Price and the product are the only two mix elements which feature significantly in strategic planning concepts.

We then observe that:

> in broad terms there are two alternatives open to the marketer – a high-price approach aimed at 'skimming the cream' off the market, and a low-price strategy aimed at pre-empting a significant share of the total market.

High-price strategies are appropriate to mature or saturated markets, which show a degree of segmentation on the basis of quality, design features and so forth, or to the introduction of a product which differs significantly from any currently available. In the case of existing markets, consumers in the higher income groups are often prepared to pay a premium for products which are differentiated from those appealing to the mass market; for example a Rolls-Royce or Toyota Lexus compared with a Renault or a Ford Escort. Owing to the limited demand at the higher prices, a small, high-quality producer can maintain a profitable level of sales without building up a sufficiently large market share to attract the competition of firms catering to the mass market. This does not mean that the latter type of firm will not diversify into the high-price segment to make fuller use of its resources, as did Ford with its purchase of Jaguar, but the established reputation of the quality producer will provide a high degree of protection against such competition.

Skimming the market is also attractive to the firm with a new and unique product. As noted earlier, new product development invariably represents a considerable investment on the part of the innovator, and a high initial price offers the opportunity to limit the costs of launching the product into the market while earning monopoly profits. A good example of such a strategy is the launching of the Polaroid Land camera, which was originally put on the market at a price of around £100, with very limited distribution and promotion. The novelty of a camera which could produce a finished print within a matter of seconds attracted a lot of free publicity, as well as being something of a symbol because of its price. As demand at the initial high price was exhausted, Polaroid lowered prices and 'slid down the demand curve', with the result that a basic camera is now available at around £10. It is interesting to note that in the USA, where the camera was developed and first put on sale, a rather different strategy was adopted and the camera offered originally at a relatively low price. The reasoning in this instance was that the purchase of a camera tends to be once and for all, whereas there is a continuing market for film, thus the more cameras that were sold the greater would be the demand for film. As the film was unique and protected by patents, other manufacturers such as Eastman-Kodak were precluded and the approach offered greater long-run profitability, provided sufficient cameras could be sold.

When adopting a skimming strategy, with the intention of subsequently reducing price to appeal to a wider market, it is important not to create ill will by reducing price too quickly. This danger may be reduced by differentiating the appearance of the product and offering it as a 'stripped-down', or economy model. The use of this strategy is to be seen in the marketing of PCs and electronic calculators, as well as camcorders, mobile phones, and so on.

A low-price policy recommends itself in a number of circumstances, pre-eminent among which is entering a market with a high price elasticity of demand. The newcomer will have to achieve a certain level of sales in order to break even and in the short run may only be able to wrest sales from existing products through the medium of an attractive discount on current prices. Penetration pricing, as this strategy is sometimes termed, usually involves the firm in accepting a loss initially, while achieving sampling of the product and the development of brand loyalty. As suggested earlier, however, few firms are willing to buy market share openly for fear of setting off a price war, and a penetration policy is usually disguised as some form of sales promotion, for example price-off labels, coupons, and so on. Where the firm possesses a cost advantage it has little to fear from a low-price strategy, but it is rare that a new entrant into a market can undercut the existing brand leaders owing to the economies of scale open to them. In fact, contrary to popular belief, oligopolists often practise a low-price policy to discourage the entry of new competitors into the market.

The arguments for skimming and penetration strategies are admirably summarized by Simon in Table 7.6.

Based on the foregoing review, now complete Exercise 7.6.

Table 7.6 Skimming vs penetration pricing

Skimming strategy	Penetration strategy
• High short-run profits little affected by discounting.	• High total contribution through fast sales growth in spite of low unit contribution margins.
• Quick pay-back for real innovation during the period of monopolistic market position, reduces long-run competitive risk, quick amortization of R&D expenses.	• Takes advantage of positive intrapersonal (durable goods) carryover effects, builds up a strong market position (with the potential of higher prices and/or higher sales in the future).
• High profit in early life-cycle phases, reduces the risk of obsolescence.	• Takes advantage of short-run cost reductions through (static) economies of scale.
• Allows for price reduction over time.	• Allows for fast increase of the cumulative quality by accelerating the experience curve effect. Achieves a large cost advantage that competitors will find difficult to match.
• Avoids the necessity of price increases.	
• High price implies positive prestige and quality.	• Reduces the risk of failure; low introductory price gives some assurance of low probability of failure.
• Requires fewer financial resources.	• Deters potential competitors from market entry, or delays their entry.
• Requires lower capacity.	

Exercise 7.6 Pricing policy and methods

1 What are the key issues influencing your pricing decision?

2 What is your pricing objective(s)? Why?

3 How important is price in your marketing mix? Why? (Remember the demand curve and price elasticity)

4 What basic strategy – skimming or penetration – do you follow? Why?

5 To what extent are your pricing methods influenced by cost, by demand, by competition? What is the relative influence of these three forces?

6 What is your preferred pricing method? Why?

Distribution policy

Distribution is a key policy area in the formulation of marketing strategy. There are only two basic strategic options with regard to a distribution policy – seek to work closely with intermediaries or else assume their functions and 'push' the product through the channel, or seek to establish a franchise with ultimate consumers and so 'pull' the product through the channel. (See earlier description of these two strategies.)

When selecting a channel for distribution, you must pay particular attention to the environmental situation, to the product and market characteristics and the company's own strengths and weaknesses. Table 7.7 summarizes the major points to be considered, most of which will have been covered in previous sections of the book.

Table 7.7 Factors influencing distribution policy

Environmental	
Market structure	● number and location of both suppliers and users
Market conduct	● degree of concentration and nature of competition
Market performance	
Legislation/regulation	
Institutional infrastructure	● what channels are available and what are their distinguishing characteristics
Product characteristics	● class of product
	● bulk/volume
	● price/value
	● durability/perishability
	● seasonality
	● service requirements
Market characteristics	● benefits looked for
	● geographic location
	● discernible segments
Company's strengths and weaknesses	● size
	● competitive standing
	● goodwill – how much, with whom
	● service and technical abilities

Once these factors have been considered, you must then consider the relative merits of the three basic strategies: undifferentiated, differentiated and concentrated marketing. However, these strategies have associated distribution strategies – intensive, selective and exclusive distribution. In *Marketing Strategy and Management* we describe these as follows.

As we have seen, an undifferentiated strategy rests on the assumption of user homogeneity and/or an implicit acceptance that we have no prior ability to segment a market and so must appeal to all of it. Either way, maximum distributive coverage is called for that almost invariably will require use of the services of intermediaries to secure it.

By contrast, differentiated marketing implies an ability to segment a market and to cater for the varying needs of the different segments. In these circumstances some segments are likely to be much more important to a given producer than others, and so justify a direct approach, while intermediaries may be used to reach more dispersed segments or those with particular needs best served by another channel member, e.g. a manufacturer of industrial equipment might sell direct to major users and through distributors or agents to increase geographical coverage. Finally, concentrated marketing calls for highly selective distribution. It also implies a smaller supplier, hence the concentration on only one segment, and so will require the use of intermediaries in all but the most geographically concentrated markets. The implications of these three strategies for distribution are summarized succinctly in J. R. Evans and B. Berman's overview of distribution planning, reproduced in Table 7.8.

Table 7.8 Intensity of channel coverage

Characteristics	Exclusive distribution	Selective distribution	Intensive distribution
Objectives	Strong image, channel control and loyalty, price stability	Moderate market coverage, solid image, some channel control and loyalty	Widespread market coverage, channel acceptance, volume sales
Channel members	Few in number, well established, reputable stores	Moderate in number, well established, better stores	Many in number, all types of outlets
Customers	Few in number, trend-setters, willing to travel to store, brand-loyal	Moderate in number, brand-conscious, somewhat willing to travel to store	Many in number, convenience-orientated
Marketing emphasis	Personal selling, pleasant shopping conditions, good service	Promotional mix, pleasant shopping conditions, good service	Mass advertising, nearby location, items in stock
Examples	Automobiles, designer clothes, caviar	Furniture, clothing, watches	Groceries, household products, magazines

Source: Evans, J. R. and Berman, B. (1982). *Marketing Management.* Macmillan.

In their textbook R. M. Gaedeke and D. Tootelian (1983) provide a very useful summary table of the factors which are likely to influence the length of the channel and, therefore, the number of intermediate functions to be performed between production and consumption. These data are reproduced in Table 7.9.

Table 7.9 Summary of factors influencing channel length

Channel consideration	Favouring long channels	Favouring short channels
Market or customer characteristics		
1 Size of purchasing unit	Small	Large
2 Number of customers	Many	Few
3 Location of customers	Geographically dispersed	Geographically concentrated
4 Customer knowledge	Considerable and widely dispersed	Limited and concentrated
5 Installation and servicing assistance	None required	Help required
Producer characteristics		
1 Size of firm	Small	Large
2 Length of time in business	New to market	Old and established in the market
3 Financial resources	Limited	Abundant
4 Location to the market	Not centrally located	Centrally located
5 Control over marketing programme	Unimportant	Important
6 Overall resource position	Weak	Strong
7 Market coverage desired	Intensive	Exclusive
8 Managerial capabilities	Weak	Strong
9 Market information availability	Limited	Abundant and expensive
10 Power	Weak	Strong
11 Policy towards pushing product	Passive	Aggressive
Environmental characteristics		
1 Number of competitors	Many	Few
2 Number of resources controlled	Few	Many
3 Economic conditions	Recessionary	Booming
4 Entry and exit of producers	Easy	Limited
5 Economic customs and traditions	Stable	Dynamic
6 Location of competitors	Geographically dispersed	Geographically concentrated
7 Laws and regulations	Tight	Loose
8 Competition among customers	Weak	Strong
9 Market to be served	New	Old

continued

Channel consideration	Favouring long channels	Favouring short channels
Product characteristics		
1 Perishability	Low	High
2 Fashionability	Low	High
3 Size of product	Small	Large
4 Value of product	Low	High
5 Weight of product	Light	Heavy
6 Complexity of product	Technically simple	Technically complex
a Special knowledge for sale	None	Considerable
b Installation	Not necessary	Required
c Maintenance	Not required	Frequent or regular
d Service	Not required	Frequent or regular
7 Risk of obsolescence	Low	High
8 Age of product	Old	New
9 Production process	Standard	Custom-built
10 Order size (quantities purchased)	Small	Large
11 Appearance of product	Undifferentiated (homogeneous)	Differentiated (heterogeneous)
12 Type of product (buying characteristics)	Convenience good	Speciality good
13 Type of product (market)	Consumer good	Industry good
14 Time of purchase	Seasonal	Non-seasonal
15 Timing of purchase	Frequently	Infrequently
16 Regularity of purchase	Regular	Irregular
17 Profit margin	Low	High
18 Width of product line	Narrow	Broad
19 Availability of requirements	Delayed	Immediately
20 Number of products per line	Few	Many
21 Product lines	Unrelated	Related
22 Number of alternative uses	Many	Limited

Source: Adapted from Brady, D. L. (1978). *An Analysis of Factors Affecting the Methods of Exporting Used by Small Manufacturing Firms*. University of Alabama.

Tables 7.7, 7.8 and 7.9 should be of considerable help to you in evaluating current market structures and formulating your own distribution policy. In doing so, you will come to appreciate that devising a distribution policy invariably involves resolution of the conflicting forces of *cost* versus *control*.

A priori the existence of channels and intermediaries implies that they can perform the functions of distribution in the most cost-effective way:

● Transfer of title to the goods involved.
● Physical movement from the point of production to the point of consumption.
● Storage functions.
● Communication of information concerning the availability, characteristics and price of the goods.
● Financing of goods in transit, inventory and on purchase.

While this may be true, there is often inertia in established institutions and one way to improve your competitiveness is to break such inertia and come up with innovative solutions which offer greater value to the final customer. In doing so, you may also be able to increase your control over the distribution function and enhance the customer franchise.

Control of a distribution channel is primarily a matter of economics (cost) but is also influenced by at least three other factors:

1 Buyer–seller concentration ratios.
2 Technical complexity.
3 Service requirements.

In food retailing, recent years have seen an enormous increase in the buying power of the 'Big 5' supermarket chains who now account for over seventy per cent of all purchases. Faced with economies of scale available to these intermediaries, it is clear that only a degree of differentiation involving technical complexity and/or service requirements will enable anyone to bypass them.

In *Marketing* (1996) we offer a checklist to help inform the choice of channel:

Customer characteristics
Number of potential users.
Geographical distribution of potential users.
Frequency of purchase.
Average order size.
Distribution of users on the basis of consumption.
Relative importance of product to user; i.e. is the product an essential input from the user's point of view, or may its purchase be postponed or delayed?
Degree of user sophistication *vis-à-vis* product characteristics; i.e. does the user need technical service and, if so, what type?
Credit standing.
Preferred purchasing pattern – a single preference is unlikely to emerge owing to variations in the above factors; e.g. the need for after-sales service.
Degree of associated service requirements – both before and after the sale.

Middleman characteristics
Market coverage.
Gross margin.
Proportion of salesforce's time available for selling product.
Degree of technical expertise.
Financial strength and stability.
Stock-carrying capacity.
Servicing capacity.
Number of substitute products carried.

Company characteristics

Size – both absolute, and relative to the industry/market of which it is a member.

Financial strength.

Industry position – leader or follower?

Spatial relationship between plant(s) and major users.

Degree of technical competence.

Degree of specialization.

Breadth of product line.

Ability to provide desired services.

Environmental and competitive characteristics

The nature of seasonal, cyclical and secular trends in demand.

Degree of concentration in user industry(ies).

Nature and usage of existing distributive channels.

Extent and nature of legal restrictions and regulations.

The impact of taxation, for example on leasing.

Government procurement policy.

Consumer needs – in so far as the demand for industrial goods is derived from consumer demand, shifts in the latter will have an impact on the former.

Based on your evaluation of the above and your earlier analysis of the value chain, user needs, segmentation, targeting and positioning, you should now be able to articulate your distribution policy.

Exercise 7.7 Distribution policy

Complete this exercise by writing in your assessment for each of the factors listed. Compare this with Table 7.9 and classify each in terms of whether this favours a long- (L) or short- (S) term channel. If the majority of your answers favour long channels, then you will probably opt for *intensive distribution*. Otherwise you will need to choose between *exclusive* and *selective* distribution.

In selecting your strategy, bear in mind that success in business frequently comes from 'changing the rules of the game'. Accordingly, if you decide on a hybrid approach or one which contradicts the conventional wisdom, you should write in your reasons for doing so in the space provided.

Channel consideration	Description	Indicated channel length	
		L	S
Market or customer characteristics 1 Size of purchasing unit 2 Number of customers 3 Location of customers 4 Customer knowledge 5 Installation and servicing assistance *Producer characteristics* 1 Size of firm 2 Length of time in business 3 Financial resources 4 Location to the market 5 Control over marketing programme 6 Overall resource position 7 Market coverage desired 8 Managerial capabilities 9 Market information availability 10 Power 11 Policy toward pushing product *Environmental characteristics* 1 Number of competitors 2 Number of resources controlled 3 Economic conditions 4 Entry and exit of producers 5 Economic customs and traditions 6 Location of competitors 7 Laws and regulations 8 Competition among customers 9 Market to be served *Product characteristics* 1 Perishability 2 Fashionability 3 Size of product 4 Value of product			

Channel consideration	Description	Indicated channel length	
		L	S

5 Weight of product
6 Complexity of product
   a Special knowledge for sale
   b Installation
   c Maintenance
   d Service
7 Risk of obsolescence
8 Age of product
9 Production process
10 Order size (quantities purchased)
11 Appearance of product
12 Type of product (buying characteristics)
13 Type of product (market)
14 Time of purchase
15 Timing of purchase
16 Regularity of purchase
17 Profit margin
18 Width of product line
19 Availability of requirements
20 Number of products per line
21 Product lines
22 Number of alternative uses			

Channel length analysis indicates we should choose:

1 Long channel   ☐
2 Short channel   ☐

Our proposed distribution strategy is:

A Exclusive   ☐
B Selective   ☐
C Intensive   ☐

Our reasons for this are:

Promotion policy

For many people, promotion is marketing and marketing is seen as being concerned primarily with advertising and personal selling, which are the main elements of the promotional mix. As a student of marketing you will appreciate that this is a misconception and that promotion is no more or less important than product, price and place. Indeed in the absence of product, price and availability there would be nothing to promote.

In essence, marketing communications have two primary roles – to *inform* and to *persuade*. Impersonal methods – advertising, sales promotion and direct mail – play a mainly informational role, whereas selling and public relations are personal methods and more concerned with persuasion. As we saw earlier when reviewing buyer behaviour, there is a certain logic to the hierarchy of effects models which propose that in coming to a buying decision users move from a state of unawareness to awareness, interest, desire and action (AIDA). Impersonal communication is usually more cost-effective in achieving the objective associated with the earlier part of this process while personal selling may be necessary to 'close' the sale, especially where it involves a major outlay and the intending buyer has little or no prior experience of the product under consideration, e.g. a motor car, piece of machinery, etc. Conversely, where the price is low it may be easier to try something for yourself and then decide whether or not to repeat purchase based on direct experience rather than someone else's recommendation.

All of the books (*Marketing*, 6th edition, *Marketing Strategy and Management*, 2nd edition, *The Marketing Book*, 3rd edition, and *Strategic Marketing Management*, 2nd edition) which the book was designed to support contain extended descriptions of the various elements of the promotional submix as illustrated in Figure 7.2.

Separately and in combination, the promotional methods listed may be used to achieve one or more of seven basic promotional objectives:

1 Increase sales.
2 Maintain or improve market share.
3 Create or improve product/brand recognition, acceptance, or insistence.
4 Create a favourable climate for future sales.
5 Inform and educate the market.
6 Create a competitive difference.
7 Improve promotional efficiency.

As our model of buyer behaviour indicates, promotion will play a major role in:

1 Creating awareness.
2 Conditioning and influencing perceptions (of the facts).
3 Suggesting subjective associations and benefits which may prove determinant when the buyer is trying to discriminate between two or more objectively similar product offerings.

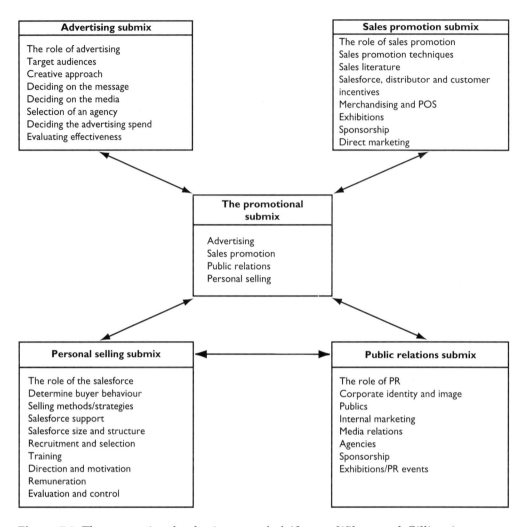

Figure 7.2 The promotional submix expanded (*Source*: Wilson and Gilligan)

Following Bell (1972), five key conditions favour the use of promotion in the marketing mix:

1 A favourable trend in demand.
2 Strong product differentiation.
3 Product qualities are hidden.
4 Emotional buying motives exist.
5 Adequate funds are available.

Once the primary objectives have been established, we can explore the various strategies available. By virtue of our preceding analysis we should have a clear idea about the market segments to be addressed and how our product is to be positioned within the chosen segment. We should also have a clear picture of the intended audience, of the benefits which are important to that audience, of their present purchasing behaviour and their reaction to price inducements. Whether through research (new market opportunity) or direct experience, we will have considerable information on the other elements of the mix.

At first sight this might seem to indicate that selecting the promotional submix should be relatively straightforward. It rarely is! For example in *Marketing Strategy and Management* we cite the case of advertising, where John O'Shaughnessy (1984) points out that with six major factors – target audience, goals (objectives), message appeal, message format, media and vehicle mix, and scheduling – and the major elements associated with each of these, there are 4320 different combinations (see Table 7.10).

If we were then to consider the sixty-three different advertising objectives listed in *Marketing Strategy and Management* in place of O'Shaughnessy's four goals, then the options would escalate to 68,040 and this is long before we begin to choose between different media.

Against this background, strategic planners must confine themselves to spelling out the primary objectives and relative emphasis to be given to the different elements of the promotional submix which might be used to achieve these. As noted, many of these will have been largely predetermined by earlier decisions.

Table 7.10 Advertising strategy

Target audience	Goals	Message appeal	Message format	Media and vehicle mix	Scheduling
Consumers/ customers	Convert	Unique selling propositions (USP)	Dogmatic	TV	Concentrated
Gatekeepers	Increase	Image	Emotional	Radio	Continuous
Opinion leaders	Attract	Positioning *vis-à-vis* competition	Reason giving	Direct advertising	Intermittent
Others	Maintain	Buying criterion Others		Magazines Newspapers Outdoor	

Source: O'Shaughnessy, John (1984). *Competitive Marketing: A Strategic Approach.* Allen & Unwin.

For example if we are introducing a unique new consumer product to the market we may have decided to target consumers with high disposable incomes with strong esteem needs. To cater to these, we have decided on high prices (a skimming strategy), exclusive distribution and a combined push and pull strategy in which intermediaries will play a major role. With this strategy personal selling in the retail outlets will be very important, so our promotional strategy will need to focus on creating awareness and interest through targeted advertising in selected media (probably specialist magazines and/or Sunday supplements), possibly direct mail and some public relations to secure endorsement and word-of-mouth recommendation.

That said, we must be wary of not becoming too dependent on 'formulaic' marketing of this kind. Remember, the overall objective is to create a sustainable competitive advantage and this may be easier to achieve by choosing a novel course of action rather than simply following the indications and prescriptions which arise from the normative theory.

Another caveat to enter here is that promotional activity can become very expensive and it is often difficult to measure specific outcomes, particularly from media advertising designed to create awareness and influence attitudes. Because of the difficulty of quantifying cause and effect, most firms adopt a simplistic approach to setting the advertising budget based on one of four methods.

- Percentage of sales.
- Competitive parity.
- What we can afford.
- Fixed sum per unit.

Any or all of these methods may be helpful in giving you some feel for the size of the promotional budget. But once you have this you will have to establish whether it will be sufficient to achieve your promotional objectives. If it is not, then you will either have to restate your objectives or find ways of allocating more money to the budget.

Against this background advice, you should now complete Exercise 7.8.

Exercise 7.8 Developing a promotional plan

Given the complexity of devising specific promotional campaigns and operational promotional plans, my colleague at Strathclyde University, Keith Crosier, has devised a checklist of information which the strategic marketing planner needs to communicate to those with specific responsibility. Answers to most of the questions will already have been formulated in completing earlier exercises, so you should focus specifically on objectives, budget, strategy and programme. Further information on how to complete the checklist is to be found in *The Marketing Book* (Baker, 1996) at p. 492 ff and *Encyclopedia of Marketing* (Baker, 1995) at p. 658 ff.

Marketing communications

The format of a marketing communications plan

1 Context Explains who and what the plan is about.

- *Raw materials*
  The product or service
  specification: what does it do?
  benefits: what does it offer?
  developments: what next?

  The company
  specification: what do we do?
  identity: who do we believe we are?
  image: how do we want to be seen?

  The audience
  demographics: where are they?
  psychographics: who are they?

  The market
  structure: what is it?
  competition: who are we up against?
  dynamics: what forecasts?

- *The marketing mix*
  What potential effect on strategies?

- *Imperatives*
  Precedents: what is traditional?
  Mandatories: what is compulsory?

2 Objectives Explains what the plan is meant to achieve.

- *Goals*
  What are the general longer-term aims?

- *Targets*
  What are the specific aims within the timescale?

- *Criteria*
  What are the benchmarks of performance?

3 Budget Explains how proposed initiatives will be paid for.

- *Appropriation*
  How much money is available to spend?

- *Allocations*
  How will it be spent?

- *Contingency*
  What if?

- *Control*
  How will budget-holder's performance be evaluated?

4 Strategy Explains how objectives are to be achieved.

- *Message*
  What do we tell the target audience?

- *Creative*
  How do we say it?

- *Vehicles*
  Which delivery systems do we use?

5 Programme Explains when initiatives will happen.

- *Timescale*
  How long have we got?

- *Schedule*
  What happens when?

6 Implementation Explains who is to put the plan into action.

- *Authority*
  Who can approve or disapprove?

- *Responsibility*
  Who co-ordinates action?

- *Delegation*
  What will be subcontracted?

- *Procedures*
  Who will keep track, and how?

Now write down your answers to the following specific questions:

1 What is our promotional objective(s)?
2 How do we intend to measure achievement of the objective?
3 What appropriation/budget is available?
4 What do we want to tell the target audience?
5 How do we propose to tell them, i.e. what vehicle or media do we intend using? What proportion of the budget will be spent on each?
6 What measures will we use to assess effectiveness of the various media?

Integrating the marketing mix

Now that we have completed our evaluation of the four key elements of the marketing mix separately, it remains to consider them as a whole to ensure that the decisions reinforce each other (synergy) and to eliminate any apparent inconsistencies. Exercise 7.9 provides a summary statement and a separate one should be completed for each product.

Exercise 7.9 Marketing mix summary

Product:				
Target market:				
Positioning statement:				
Stage in PLC:	Intro ☐	Growth ☐	Maturity ☐	Decline ☐
Core strategy:	Undifferentiated ☐	Differentiated ☐	Concentrated ☐	
Key approach:	Push ___%	Pull ___%		
Pricing:	Skimming ☐	Penetration ☐		
Distribution:	Exclusive ☐	Selective ☐	Intensive ☐	
Promotion:	Impersonal ___%	Personal ___%		

You should now complete Exercise 7.10 to help you diagnose how well you are managing the various policies at present and so identify areas for attention and improvement.

Exercise 7.10 How well are we doing?

1 **Product policy**

Overall, our management of product policy is:

Excellent	Very Good	Good	Average	Poor	Don't Know
☐	☐	☐	☐	☐	☐

2 **New product policy**

Overall, our management of new product policy is:

Excellent	Very Good	Good	Average	Poor	Don't Know
☐	☐	☐	☐	☐	☐

3 **Service policy**

Overall, our management of service policy is:

Excellent	Very Good	Good	Average	Poor	Don't Know
☐	☐	☐	☐	☐	☐

4 **Pricing policy**

Overall, our management of pricing policy is:

Excellent	Very Good	Good	Average	Poor	Don't Know
☐	☐	☐	☐	☐	☐

5 **Promotional policy**

Overall, our management of promotional policy is:

Excellent	Very Good	Good	Average	Poor	Don't Know
☐	☐	☐	☐	☐	☐

6 **Distribution policy**

Overall, our management of distribution policy is:

Excellent	Very Good	Good	Average	Poor	Don't Know
☐	☐	☐	☐	☐	☐

Developing the marketing plan

Having completed the preceding exercises, we are now in a position to synthesize our conclusions and recommendations into a coherent and integrated plan which can be communicated to others for action. Based upon observation of best practice it is generally agreed that an effective marketing plan should contain the elements listed below and that these should be presented in the sequence suggested.

The amount of detail contained in the marketing plan is very much a matter of personal preference. At one end of the spectrum we can provide a blow-by-blow account detailing the information reviewed and the interpretation placed upon it product by product and market by market in much the same manner as undertaken in the exercises. Alternatively, we may regard these as the raw materials from which we will fabricate a synoptic plan setting out the key essentials but leaving a degree of discretion to those who will be responsible for implementing the plan. As a broad generalization, the former approach is best suited to mature and declining markets, where there is a high degree of certainty about inputs and outcomes, and profits will be maximized by close attention to detail and fine-tuning to extract the maximum efficiency from the resources employed. Conversely, in dynamic growth markets, where change is frequent and largely unpredictable, line management must have the flexibility to adjust their actions to suit the circumstances as they evolve. Under these conditions the highly detailed marketing plan becomes a straightjacket, inhibiting movement and likely to lead to disaster. Accordingly, we do not prescribe any particular length for the various sections. This is a matter for your judgement based upon the specific context in which you are operating and the audience for whom you are writing the plan. That said, your plan should include the following.

Executive Summary

Background: A short description of the company, its current markets, products and performance. The purpose, structure and content of the plan.

Mission Statement

Marketing Appreciation

   A Macroenvironmental analysis
- PEST
- Key issues

B Microenvironmental analysis
- Industry/market
- Competitors
- Customers

C Self-analysis

SWOT analysis

Conclusions and Key Assumptions

Strategic Objectives

Core Strategy

Key Policies

Product
Price
Place
Promotion

Administration and Control

Communication

Timing

Summary

In this chapter we have addressed the third of our fundamental questions: 'How do I get there?'.

To begin with, we looked at the concept of the marketing mix with its four basic elements about which the strategist has to make key policy decisions and over which he or she can exercise a fairly high degree of control – product, price, place and promotion.

Next we examined each of the basic elements in some detail with a view to identifying the principal objectives that might be achieved through their use. In the process we recognized a small number of alternative strategies applicable to each as well as detecting some logical linkages in certain combinations of strategies. For example for an organization with a highly *differentiated* product but a limited production capacity, a *skimming* price strategy, *selective* distribution and print media *advertising* in specialist magazines following a mainly *push* approach would be appropriate.

However, as we pointed out, there is an almost infinite number of combinations and permutations possible given the number of variables encompassed by the 4Ps and the challenge to the planner is to come up with a unique combination which adds value and meets customer needs.

Finally, we outlined the key headings for a marketing plan. By now you have gathered most if not all the information necessary to complete such a plan as well as diagnosing those options which appear to offer the greatest opportunity to your organization. In order to operationalize such a plan a great deal more information on your specific market and the deployment of the 4Ps would be necessary. Much of this, particularly that concerned with the detailed plans for distribution and promotion, would call for specialist input, and is beyond the scope of this book. Similarly, the assignment of responsibility and implementation call for considerable elaboration in practice. For example the US Army's specification for a plan reads as follows:

Characteristics of a plan

The essential element of a plan is that it offers a definite course of action and a method for execution. A good plan:

a *Provides for accomplishing the mission.* (Does it accomplish the objective of the planning?)

b *Is based on facts and valid assumptions.* (Have all pertinent data been considered? Are the data accurate? Have assumptions been reduced to a minimum?)

c *Provides for the use of existing resources.* (Is the plan workable? Are there any resources organic to the organization that are not being fully utilized? Are there any resources available from higher headquarters that should be used?)

d *Provides the necessary organization.* (Does the plan clearly establish relationships and fix responsibilities?)

e *Provides continuity.* (Does the plan provide the organization personnel, material and arrangements for the full period of the contemplated operation?)

f *Provides decentralization.* (Does the plan delegate authority to the maximum extent consistent with the necessary control?)

g *Provides direct contact.* (Does the plan permit co-ordination during execution by direct contact between co-equals and counterparts on all levels?)

h *Is simple.* (Have all elements been eliminated that are not essential to successful action? Have all elements been reduced to their simplest forms? Have all possibilities for misunderstanding been eliminated?)

i *Is flexible.* (Does the plan leave room for adjustment to change in operating conditions? Where necessary, are alternative courses of action stipulated?)

j *Provides control.* (Do adequate means exist, or have they been provided, to insure that the plan is carried out in accordance with the commander's intent?)

k *Is co-ordinated.* (Is the plan fully co-ordinated? When appropriate, has the commander been informed of non-concurrence or non-co-ordination?)

Reproduced from FM 101–5, 14 June 1968, by permission of The Department of the Army.

In the next and final chapter we look briefly at our fourth basic question: 'How will I know when I've arrived?'.

Chapter 8

How will I know when I've arrived?

Introduction

This will be a short chapter, if for no other reason that, unless you are working on a discrete project, strategic planning is an unbroken and iterative process in which goals and objectives are continuously updated in the light of new information – what Mintzberg terms 'emergent strategy'. Competition is a dynamic state in which the players seek to outmanoeuvre their competitors and change the behaviour of customers and users. Innovation is all. It would be surprising if the strategic planner were not to be faced with a state of flux and change.

But, as pointed out earlier, if we have no concept of a destination we will have no way of knowing if we have made any progress. Using a sailing analogy, if you are out of the sight of land and surrounded by a featureless sea, then you need a measurement system (latitude, longitude and charts) to establish where you are in relation to where you want to be, as well as a compass to ensure you are travelling in the right direction. In strategic planning for business the plan specifies where we want to be, the direction to take (objectives and strategies) and a large number of checkpoints against which we can measure progress. Because of the legal requirement that organizations must make a formal statement of their financial affairs on an annual basis to establish their liability for taxes and to confirm that they are solvent and trading legally, most progress measures are summarized in an annual budget. This budget is then disaggregated into smaller time units (days, weeks and months) for closer monitoring and control. The development of forecasts, budgets and day-to-day control measures of this kind is beyond the scope of this book. In this chapter we look at three topics which are valuable in charting overall progress without going into the detail appropriate for tactical control purposes. These topics are: project planning, critical path analysis and the measurement and control of marketing effectiveness.

Project planning

During the 1980s the forces of increased global competition, accelerating technological change and worldwide recession resulted in major changes in organizational structures. 'Buzz' phrases of the era included 'Business Process Re-engineering', 'Downsizing' and 'Empowerment'. Collectively, these supposedly new approaches to management reflected a recognition that many organizations had become overly hierarchical, bureaucratized and centralized. In the process new specialist functions such as strategic planning and marketing had emerged, insulating those with responsibility and authority from issues of operationalization and implementation. The result was that senior management lost touch with their customers. The solution was to re-establish contact by stripping out unnecessary layers of management and pushing authority down the organization to empower those with direct responsibility for delivering value to the customers. In the process it was rediscovered that people work better when they can identify closely with the operational unit and be measured against its performance rather than that of some larger, monolithic enterprise of which it is only a minor part.

To achieve the benefits of adaptability and flexibility enjoyed by SMEs, many large organizations have adopted a project approach whereby teams of people are assembled to plan and execute specific tasks. A review of a number of project planning manuals identified twenty-four management activities involved in designing and implementing a successful project. These activities are listed in random order in Exercise 8.1. Your task, as with the critical success factors exercise, is to rank order them in *sequence*, with 1 being the first task to be completed and 24 the last. As before, you can do this as either an individual or group exercise. The experts' rankings are on page 222 and represent a consensus of the optimal sequence.

Exercise 8.1 Project planning and implementation

Management activities	Step 1 – Individual ranking	Step 2 – Team ranking	Step 3 – Experts' ranking	Step 4 – Difference between steps 1 and 3	Step 5 – Difference between steps 2 and 3
A Establish milestones to assess progress					
B Make necessary adjustments to plan					
C Train personnel for new appointments					
D Identify possible courses of action					
E Establish current position					
F Define the problem to be addressed					
G Reward/correct/punish individual performance					
H Define acceptable variances from planned performance					
I Agree individual performance objectives					
J Estimate outcomes for each course of action					
K Collect additional data					
L Develop a strategy					
M Assign authority, responsibility and accountability					
N Specify the precise tasks to be performed					
O Set objectives					
P Appraise individual performance					
Q Select qualified personnel					
R State assumptions					
S Select preferred course of action					
T Initiate project					
U Determine additional information needs					
V Assess progress against agreed milestones/targets					
W Spell out desired organizational structure					
X Allocate resources					
Totals (the lower the score the better)					
				Individual score Step 4	Team score Step 5

Critical path analysis

Listing the tasks to be performed in an optimal sequence enables you to develop a critical path. Critical path analysis (CPA) and its associate, programme evaluation and review technique (PERT), were developed by the US military to improve the efficiency and effectiveness of planning, co-ordinating, implementing and controlling complex tasks. Unfortunately, like the precepts of quality assurance and management which were developed at the same time, CPA and PERT have been sadly neglected in modern management practice. Indeed while CPA (or CPM – critical path method) and PERT are frequently referred to as key elements in systems thinking and network analysis, few authors of management or marketing texts offer any explanation of the term. Older texts (1960s and 1970s) on operations management are more forthcoming.

In *The Product Planning System* (1967), Lewis N. Goslin points out that CPM and PERT:

> were designed to evaluate project progress, focus attention on problems in the program, and provide management with information through status reports. In addition, they display information on the likelihood of reaching project objectives and determine the shortest time in which a subject can be completed. A program plan is the sequential list of events necessary to achieve the stated goal; therefore, where critical path planning is utilized, it is necessary for these events to be stated in such an order that all significant relationships can be recognized. (p. 79)

Strategically, the key skill is to identify the events and the sequence in which they need to be completed. For example, Hart and Baker (1986) used the CPM as the organizing principle for developing their multiple convergent processing model for new product development, as illustrated in Figure 8.1.

Irrespective of the level of detail in our operational marketing plan, its overall achievement will depend upon the completion of numerous sub-tasks and their associated sub-objectives. In order to construct an overall critical path for the implementation of the marketing plan it will be necessary first to develop critical paths for the component parts or sub-systems. To give you some insight into what is involved you should now complete Exercise 8.2, which requires you to develop a critical path for the development and launch of a new product. To begin with, list the key events, activities and resources you consider necessary. Next, list these in chronological order with timings and start and completion dates (remember you can progress tasks simultaneously and in parallel). Finally, chart these as a critical path.

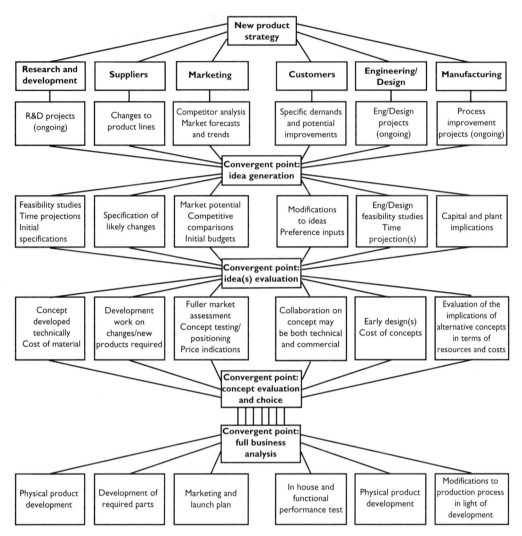

Figure 8.1 The multiple convergent process (*Source*: Hart, S.J. and Baker, M.J. (1994) 'Multiple convergent processing', *International Marketing*, 11(1), 77–92)

Exercise 8.2 Developing a critical path for a new product

1 List the key events, activities and resources involved:

2 Order your list chronologically with timings and start and finish requirements:

Factor	Time required	Start	Finish

3 Plot your data as a critical path:

Exercise 8.3 Measurement, feedback and control

Following is a list of activities undertaken by organizations to measure and control marketing effectiveness.

You are asked:

1 To rate the priority of each activity as high, medium or low *in its relevance to your organization's success in the marketplace*.
2 Having identified those activities which are relevant to your operation – exclude those you have rated 'low' – *rate the effectiveness of the systems your organization uses to measure and monitor that marketing activity*.

Please rate both the priority and the competence rating *as you perceive it as it actually is, and not as it should be.*

The 'organization' you are rating may not be the whole company but that part of it in which you operate.

As with all the other checklists and exercises, this is illustrative rather than comprehensive. Your organization may consider other measures more relevant than those listed, in which case you should construct your own pro forma. Given that the objective is to establish *perceptions* and *judgements*, the real value lies in comparing these with other people to create a consensus view and implement any changes indicated by the analysis.

Activity	1 Priority			2 Competence					
	High	Med	Low	Very competent					Very incompetent
(a) Planning/Product									
1 Long-term (3+ years) review of *current markets*	1	1	0	1	2	3	4	5	6
2 Long-term review of *current products* (major money-spinners)	1	1	0	1	2	3	4	5	6
3 New product-developing market plans	1	1	0	1	2	3	4	5	6
4 Long-term review of *potential* new markets/products	1	1	0	1	2	3	4	5	6
5 Annual marketing plan for all major products/ranges	1	1	0	1	2	3	4	5	6
(b) Price–Costs									
6 Systematic competitor price monitoring	1	1	0	1	2	3	4	5	6
7 Cost monitoring (routine value analysis?)	1	1	0	1	2	3	4	5	6
8 Systematic price–cost–profit control	1	1	0	1	2	3	4	5	6
9 Systematic monitoring of discounts given to customers	1	1	0	1	2	3	4	5	6

Activity	1 Priority			2 Competence					
	High	Med	Low	Very competent					Very incompetent
(c) Selling									
10 Annual review of salesforce/selling strategy	I	I	0	1	2	3	4	5	6
11 Systematic and detailed sales order analysis	I	I	0	1	2	3	4	5	6
12 Annual 'Key Account' customer reviews	I	I	0	1	2	3	4	5	6
13 Cost-effectiveness analysis of customers called on	I	I	0	1	2	3	4	5	6
14 Control mechanisms on 'special' discounts	I	I	0	1	2	3	4	5	6
15 Annual review of salesforce's selling aids	I	I	0	1	2	3	4	5	6
(d) Promotion									
16 Annual planning of all promotional activities: advertising, PR, exhibitions, mail shots, etc.	I	I	0	1	2	3	4	5	6
17 Routine monitoring of competitor's promotional activity	I	I	0	1	2	3	4	5	6
18 Routine monitoring of promotional expenditure budgets	I	I	0	1	2	3	4	5	6
19 Ad agency/PR agency review systems	I	I	0	1	2	3	4	5	6
(e) Distribution/Channels									
20 Annual analysis of physical distribution effectiveness	I	I	0	1	2	3	4	5	6
21 Regular cost analysis of distribution service levels (guaranteed delivery time of routine orders, damaged stock policy, etc.)	I	I	0	1	2	3	4	5	6
22 Distribution (agent, retailer, wholesaler) effectiveness monitoring: pricing, display, stock levels, product range carried, etc.	I	I	0	1	2	3	4	5	6
23 Debtor-control systems	I	I	0	1	2	3	4	5	6
24 Credit-rating systems	I	I	0	1	2	3	4	5	6
(f) Market information									
25 Product acceptability data from end-user. Your products *and* your competitors	I	I	0	1	2	3	4	5	6
26 Market profiles of end-users (demographics, etc.)	I	I	0	1	2	3	4	5	6
27 Regular sales (volume and value) information for total market and market segments (annually, quarterly *or* monthly)	I	I	0	1	2	3	4	5	6
(g) Revenue management									
28 Routine review (monthly?) of progress of revenue and profits, product (range) by product	I	I	0	1	2	3	4	5	6

Postscript

You will recall from the Preface that we set out with three basic objectives:

1 To test the user's understanding of key concepts and practices.
2 To reinforce learning by applying the knowledge base to the solution of practical problems.
3 To develop skills and competences in problem solving and communication and, particularly, in the specification, diagnosis and solution of marketing problems.

If you have worked through the text methodically you will have developed a strategic marketing plan for your organization (or the Barnstaple Company). Converting this to an operational plan will require more work but you should now have a robust and internally consistent framework from which to work and the confidence with which to repeat the exercise. Good luck!

Appendix A

Solutions to exercises

Chapter 3

Exercise 3.1 What business are we in?

One reason for choosing the Barnstaple Company as a case study to exemplify the use of the book is that it manufactures and sells a product we are all familiar with – a diary. It follows that all of us will have ideas about the needs which a diary satisfies and the benefits we (and others) get from owning and using one. We may also be able to identify other needs and benefits which a diary may fulfil for other people. So, to answer the question: 'What business are we in?', we should list all the different categories of user that we can think of together with the associated needs/benefits. Your list might look something like the following:

User	Needs/benefits
Individual	Personal record system Planner Aide-mémoire Information source Gift
Organization	Membership record Information source Promotional tool Corporate gift

You will recall that the needs served must be identified to avoid marketing myopia – a failure to consider future products which may offer improved and better ways of meeting the need and which may be preferred as a substitute.

But in addition to considering the user/consumer, we also need to take account of the producer's needs and objectives.

In the short to medium term the producer is limited by the nature of both its physical and human assets as well as by its relationship with suppliers and customers. While some plant and equipment may be put to other uses, other plant and equipment may be so specialized that it can only be used for the specific purpose for which it was designed. Clearly the more specialized your physical assets the longer it will take to recoup their value and re-invest in new resources.

Much the same applies to the skills and competences of the firm's workforce. Some personnel may be trained and reskilled very quickly while others will need much longer.

It follows that we should also define the business in terms of its technology and skills and that these need to be evaluated in terms of the value chain of which the firm is a member. (You will remember that a value chain describes the flow of goods and services from primary production through to final consumption and after-sales service, identifying who is involved and where value is added in the process.)

Thinking about the Barnstaple Company, the most relevant section of their value chain might look as shown in Figure A.1.

From this value chain we might conclude that in the short to medium term the Barnstaple Company may be described as a specialized printer/binder supplying paper-based products to both organizational and individual buyers.

Its immediate problem arises from the fact that its products are highly seasonal in nature. This means that they have to be manufactured well in advance of sale and then put into stock. The actual selling season is very short and the product becomes worthless within a few weeks of the start of the year for which it was produced. In helping to diagnose Barnstaple's problem we will return to these factors again. Similarly, looking to the longer term we may perceive electronic notebooks and palmtop computers as a major threat to the diary, so that when developing a strategy we will need to explore how our

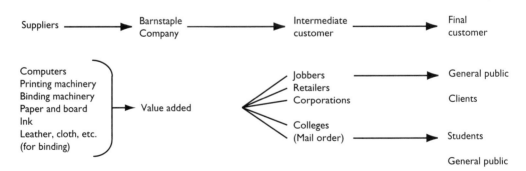

Figure A1 Barnstaple Company value chain

current definition of the company and its assets and skills may be deployed to best effect.

In considering the nature of the value chain we also need to consider how changes in the ultimate customers' needs will impact on the intermediaries who are our major customers and what they might do in response to these changes. Similarly, how will changes in our need affect our suppliers and what may they do to help us respond to these changes? We return to all these questions in later exercises.

It is hoped that this basic diagnosis of how to address the question: 'What business are we in?' will be useful in helping to indicate what issues and factors you should consider in evaluating a company of your choice. In the final analysis, the answer to such a basic question must be a matter of individual perception and judgement. If your organization has a formal statement concerning its business, then you will need to compare this with your own diagnosis and be able to justify any differences between them. Even more important, if you are a member of a management team you will need to discuss your analysis with your colleagues and see if you can agree a consensus of the issues concerned.

Exercise 3.2 How marketing orientated are you?

Below we present the pro forma as it might have been completed by someone with a marketing orientation. Alongside each attitude statement we have indicated the orientation which 'Strongly Agree' reflects, i.e.:

T = Technological
P = Production
F = Finance
S = Sales
M = Marketing

As you can see, some attitude statements reflect more than one orientation although all the marketing statements are unequivocal. You will also note that a marketer would only have some measure of agreement with one non-marketing statement – number 1. The reason why we agree that the sales force should be expected to sell what the factory can make is that a major function of the sales force is to act as a 'buffer' between the organization and the marketplace in the short term. If marketing has done its job properly, then the factory should be making what the market wants. But, as tastes change, demand for the old product will slacken and the production function may need some help from sales to manage the decline phase as it switches resources to a replacement product.

To interpret your own answers you should regard Technological and Production as one orientation, as are Sales, Finance and Marketing. In summary, the answers which reflect these are:

Technological/Production:	1, 8, 9, 11, 12, 15, 16, 18, 19, 24, 26, 28
Finance:	2, 5, 7, 11, 17, 21
Sales:	3, 6, 10, 12, 14, 15, 20, 23
Marketing:	4, 13, 22, 25, 27

If you find yourself in agreement with the majority of statements in one of these clusters, then this reflects your basic orientation.

With regard to the Barnstaple Company, the three functional managers are really caricatures of their orientation. Thus the accountant wants to drop both the college and novelty lines because (according to his accounts) they are not making profits. The sales manager clearly accepts the accountant's financial view because he wants to drop the college lines, which show an actual loss on paper whereas the novelty lines are at break-even. He also defends the novelty lines on the grounds that they earn a higher margin and because they cater to customer needs for a differentiated product. Finally, the production manager wants to drop the novelty lines because, by inference, they disrupt the production line schedules with short runs. He also claims that he's not to blame for the unsold stock of college lines (he is!), implying it was sales that got the forecast wrong.

As we shall see in our later analysis, all three functional managers are coming to wrong conclusions because their perception of the facts is distorted to some degree by their orientation.

		Strongly agree	Agree	Disagree	Strongly disagree
	IN MY ORGANIZATION:				
P	1. The sales force is expected to sell what the factory can make.	☐	☑	☐	☐
F	2. There is an emphasis on short-term profits at the expense of long-term success in the marketplace.	☐	☐	☑	☐
S	3. We believe customers must get what they want, even if it is rather unprofitable for the company.	☐	☐	☐	☑
M	4. The business is committed to a long-term strategic point of view, supported by thorough market planning.	☑	☐	☐	☐

Continued

		Strongly agree	Agree	Disagree	Strongly disagree
F	5. We focus primarily on the bottom line and productivity, and only then on the customer and the marketplace.	☐	☐	☐	☑
S	6. Subjective sales-force forecasts largely determine the production process.	☐	☐	☑	☐
F	7. We base the price of our products on cost only, worked out by the accountants, who dictate pricing strategy almost regardless of the marketplace.	☐	☐	☐	☑
T	8. Research and engineering are the heart of the business and our marketing people are not usually involved in determining what products we should make.	☐	☐	☑	☐
P	9. The factory floor is the focal centre of the organization.	☐	☐	☐	☑
S	10. Productivity improvements often result in changes to product specification which make the product difficult to sell to the customer.	☐	☐	☐	☑
F/T/P	11. Capital investment decisions which involve new technology and the relocation of manufacturing plant rarely involve the marketing people.	☐	☐	☑	☐
P/S	12. We believe that selling volume comes first. Profits then generally follow.	☐	☐	☐	☑
M	13. We believe in the principle of managing the marketplace, by expecting – and managing – change.	☑	☐	☐	☐

Continued

		Strongly agree	Agree	Disagree	Strongly disagree
S	14. We tend to fit our forecasts to the profits that we know are expected of us; then we plan how to achieve the forecast.	☐	☐	☑	☐
T/S/P	15. We don't pay a lot of attention to market research.	☐	☐	☑	☐
P	16. Product planning takes place on the factory floor, not in the marketing department.	☐	☐	☐	☑
F	17. Product costs, consumer prices and the whole panoply of customer-service expenditure tends to be based on profit needs, not market needs.	☐	☐	☐	☑
P	18. We tend to see ourselves as manufacturers rather than as marketers.	☐	☐	☐	☑
T	19. Our R&D people don't spend much time talking to the sales and marketing people.	☐	☐	☑	☐
S	20. If customers aren't happy with our products, we tend to go looking for new customers rather than new products.	☐	☐	☐	☑
F	21. We tend to be more concerned with return on investment in the short term, than with customer satisfaction in the long term.	☐	☐	☑	☐
M	22. Our focus is on the marketplace: identifying customer needs and meeting those needs – profitably.	☑	☐	☐	☐
S	23. Our sales people are given great freedom in pricing, servicing and credit terms.	☐	☐	☐	☑

Continued

		Strongly agree	Agree	Disagree	Strongly disagree
T/P	24. The product is the concern of our technical people, with little input from the marketing people.	☐	☐	☑	☐
M	25. The emphasis is on a balance between market share, market status and long-term profitability.	☑	☐	☐	☐
T/P	26. Marketing guidance for the engineers and the production people is often weak or non-existent.	☐	☐	☑	☐
M	27. We work with a lot of information feedback systems from the marketplace to measure and guide our activities.	☑	☐	☐	☐
T/P	28. We tend to over-engineer our products way past the point of customer need – and his or her ability to pay.	☐	☐	☑	☐

Chapter 4

Exercise 4.1 Competitive critical success factors

This is the first of several exercises using a factor rating table of the kind described in Chapter 2. You were presented with three lists of factors which research has indicated are influential in coming to a decision. The first list contains sixteen product factors influencing competitiveness, followed by eleven management factors influencing competitiveness and seven factors influencing the design and development of new products. Because the tables were presented to you in this order, experience shows that ninety-nine per cent of those completing the exercise will have completed them in the same sequence when it would have been simpler to take them in *reverse* order, i.e. 'solve' the simplest problem first. (Check back; no one said the problems had to be tackled in a given order. The instruction was to solve all the problems.) This is especially true of the group exercises, where the team has to agree on *how* to address the problem before actually solving it – the less the complexity (fewer factors to consider) the more likely the team will come up with an effective approach.

If you are doing the exercise on your own, then compare your answers with the experts' ratings entered into column 3 and then compute the difference between your answer and the expert answer. Don't bother with positive or negative signs; simply sum the differences and enter the total at the bottom of column 4. The smaller the total the more closely your answer agrees with the expert answer. That said, you should not worry unduly if your ranking of the product factors varies significantly even though you were asked to evaluate a particular product. If everyone was looking for the same features in a car, we would have fewer manufacturers and a standard model!

However, in the case of the management and new product development factors the experts' rankings do reflect best practice, so you should think carefully if your answer is significantly different from theirs.

The real value of this exercise comes from group problem solving. In the real world managers usually work as members of a team and shared commitment to, and responsibility for, a decision is often more important than the actual decision itself. As we observed in Chapter 2, if there are objectively correct answers to a problem then you don't need expensive managers offering judgements of what it ought to be. So if you are the member of a group seeking to achieve a consensus, how should you set about the task?

Whether you know group members well or are meeting for the first time, the first thing to do is appoint a chair and a secretary. A chair is necessary to help structure the process, to ensure that all points of view are considered, to adjudicate if necessary and to ensure that the task is completed within the time allowed. A secretary is necessary to keep a record of the proceedings, of the conclusions drawn and the decisions made. If the group has to make a formal report, then it is the secretary who will draft this.

Once a chair has been appointed, the next task is to agree what is the problem to be solved – in this case to rank order the three sets of factors – and what procedure is to be followed. The first decision should be to tackle the easiest, seven-factor problem first so that the group can get to know each other and work out a *modus operandi*. Second, you should share the data by creating a matrix with columns for the factors and individuals and rows for the individual scores for each factor. If you have a board, flipchart or OHP, then one summary sheet can be constructed for all – otherwise make up your own summary table. Now everyone has *all* the information. Usually someone will say: 'My number 1 is ... What's yours?', often resulting in as many different answers as there are group members. If you have a data matrix, simple inspection will help you to reduce the data to more manageable proportions. For example answers will often cluster into those considered very important (low scores) and those which are relatively unimportant (high scores) with something of a mish-mash in the middle. If this is the case, then you can focus on the clusters.

Once you've clustered the data, most groups will then average the scores – indeed many groups average the scores as a means of creating their cluster. In the absence of any other organizing principle averaging is as good a procedure as any, provided you don't just accept the result which is a satisficing solution. For example if there are six group members, and three rank design 1 and three rank it 16, then the average is 8, which is clearly unsatisfactory to everyone as views are strongly polarized on the issue. This is an extreme example, but underlines the point that group decisions are usually better than individual answers (compare individual and group scores with the experts) because they draw on more knowledge and experience. Creating the matrix and averaging are means of highlighting where agreement and disagreement exist – this is the problem to be solved.

If conflict (disagreement) exists, there are three broad approaches to solving it:

1 Smoothing (or satisficing) – accept the averages at face value. The easy way out.
2 Forcing. I'm the chair, do as I say.
3 Problem solving or negotiation. There are clear differences in members' views – let's ask them to explain the thinking behind their score and see if we can reach a joint agreement.

In exercises such as this the problem-solving approach frequently shows that disagreement arises from language, meaning and ambiguity. The words are the same but have different connotations for different individuals. If this is so, then all we have to do is agree how we are going to define, say, the difference between design and appearance. More basic differences may arise because of the background and orientation of group members. But, having defined your business from the perspectives of the customer's needs and diagnosed your basic orientation, you should now be able to take a more objective view and help your colleagues to reach a real consensus.

In respect of the Barnstaple Company then, the expert answers on the managerial factors and new product development apply to them. In terms of the product characteristics, however, we need to remind ourselves that different customers may well rank order the factors quite differently. For example design might be the number one consideration for someone selecting a diary for a gift. Further, how does design differ from performance in use for a product such as a diary?

As we have said before, there is no right answer. What is important for James Barnstaple is that he identifies his customer groups and then gets his management team to rank order their perceptions of the importance of the factors and negotiate an agreement along the lines summarized above.

Product factors influencing competitiveness	Stage 1 – Individual ranking	Stage 2 – Team ranking	Stage 3 – Experts' ranking	Stage 4 – Difference between stages 1 and 3	Stage 5 – Difference between stages 2 and 3
a. Style/fashion			16		
b. Durability			7		
c. Flexibility and adaptability of the product in use			13		
d. Parts availability and cost			11		
e. Attractive appearance/shape			12		
f. Technical sophistication			5		
g. Performance in operation			1		
h. Ease of use			8		
i. Sale price			3		
j. Safety in use			9		
k. Reliability			2		
l. Ease of maintenance			10		
m. Quality of after-sales service			6		
n. Efficient delivery			4		
o. Advertising and promotion			14		
p. Operator comfort			15		
				Total	Total

Management factors influencing competitiveness	Stage 1 – Individual ranking	Stage 2 – Team ranking	Stage 3 – Experts' ranking	Stage 4 – Difference between stages 1 and 3	Stage 5 – Difference between stages 2 and 3
a. Willingness to enter into collaborative arrangements			10		
b. Readiness to carry out in-depth research before entering new markets			7		
c. Readiness to adopt modern techniques (e.g. CAD, CAM, FMS, robotization, quality circles, etc.)			8		
d. Readiness to look far ahead into the future			9		
e. Close co-operation between research and development, production and marketing			4		
f. Effective management of design and innovation			3		
g. Effective use of ideas derived from the market			5		
h. Effective use of ideas derived from technology			6		
i. Clear objectives			2		
j. Top management support			1		
k. Government support			11		
				Total	Total

Factors influencing the design and development of new products	Stage 1 – Individual ranking	Stage 2 – Team ranking	Stage 3 – Experts' ranking	Stage 4 – Difference between stages 1 and 3	Stage 5 – Difference between stages 2 and 3
a. The authority/power of the person directing a project			1		
b. The product has a higher technological content than rival product offerings			3		
c. Close interaction with customers/users during the stages of design and development			2		
d. Continuous product reviews during and after product design and development in the light of changes in the environment			4		
e. Extensive use of new and improved manufacturing techniques			5		
f. Product is designed and developed by a team of qualified engineering and industrial designers			7		
g. Designers see the product through to commercialization			6		
				Total	Total

Chapter 5

Exercises 5.1, 5.2 and 5.3 Macroenvironmental analysis

As we noted in Chapter 5, the importance of macroenvironmental analysis is that it defines the threats and opportunities facing the firm both now and in the future. Three exercises were provided to help you to summarize your views on these. Exercise 5.1 (PEST analysis) and Exercise 5.2 (Cross-impact matrix) are designed to help managers identify and share what they consider to be the key issues in respect of their own organization. Obviously, if you are James Barnstaple running a small domestic business in a specialized niche market, a very broad-brush analysis will suffice. If you work for Shell, ICI or Glaxo Wellcome, a detailed global and country-by-country analysis will be called for. The key point about the exercises is to get you to formalize, communicate and share your views on the matter. Thus, James Barnstaple and his team might have come up with a simple PEST analysis such as the one shown below.

Political factors	Economic factors
1 EU legislation? ● Minimum wages ● Materials usage ● Health and safety	1 Increasing prosperity
2	2 More/longer full-time education
3	3 Contained growth of service industries
4	4 Extended (EU) market
Social factors	**Technological factors**
1 More leisure time	1 Electronic data storage ● Palmtop computers ● Voice recognition ● Smart cards
2 'High-touch' (more social exchange/gift giving)	2 Mobile communications
3 Environmentalism	3

Given the nature of their business Barnstaple seem unlikely to be affected by political factors although there is an off-chance that EU legislation might require them to modify work practices which could have a negative impact on the business. On the economic front, the signs are positive and suggest increased market opportunities – particularly the expansion of higher education. Similarly, the social trends suggest opportunities arising from the growth of social institutions (membership benefits) and gift giving. The emphasis on relationships and loyalty schemes also creates opportunities for corporate gift giving. However, environmentalism and a reduced consumption of paper- (wood)-based materials may have a negative impact.

Finally, the technological trends are all negative in the long run. Bearing in mind Levitt's marketing myopia (what business are we in?), can we realistically play a role in an electronic future? Certainly not as manufacturers; possibly as assemblers but more likely as distributors of the alternative products to our current customer base if we can add value for both the manufacturers and our customers.

QUEST would be overkill for Barnstaple, but if you're working as a group, then the individual PEST analyses provide the basis for this analysis.

The ETOM exercise (5.3) is different in that you have been provided with a list of secular trends and have been asked to rate and score these. No solution is offered for this exercise. It is your answer that matters. That said, if you are working with an instructor or consultant they may well want to question and critique your answer.

Exercises 5.4 to 5.10 Microenvironmental and self-analysis

The remaining exercises in Chapter 5 relate to the organization's task environment and its own strengths and weaknesses compared with this.

Exercise 5.4 invites you to identify the factors critical to success in your own industry/market. As noted, the critical success factors (CSF) are basically independent of the firm in the sense that they define those activities or attributes which are necessary conditions for survival in a particular market. It follows that your list depends on the markets you serve. James Barnstaple might have come up with a list such as this:

1 Existing customer base/relationships.
2 Design capability.
3 Procurement skills.
4 Manufacturing efficiency.

Diaries are a low-tech product. Many printing firms could easily produce them. Indeed they probably have the advantage over Barnstaple in that they can treat them as a seasonal line and so do not face the inventory problems of a specialist manufacturer. In such a market differentiation and customer relationships are essential to survival. To sustain their distinctiveness and add value the ability to design to meet customer specification would probably rank second (performance), with cost-benefit depending on procurement and manufacturing skills coming next.

As we have no competitor data in the case we cannot complete this part of the exercise but some desk research might allow you to benchmark other established suppliers such as Letts.

The next step, covered by Exercise 5.5, is to assess what skills and competences the organization has which distinguish it from the competition and are the source of a sustainable competitive advantage. For many firms in mature industries such as Barnstaple, the only real source of advantage may be their existing relationship with their customers. To sustain this they will have to pay continuous attention to the CSF and benchmark their competitors' activity to ensure that they can match if not beat the competition.

For firms with products in the introductory or growth phases of the life cycle, other sources of competitive advantage will be important as firms jockey for position and seek to win new customers entering the market. Clarifying such skills and competences will be greatly assisted by completing Exercise 5.6, which invites us to summarize the needs of customers in the different segments. For Barnstaple you should complete an analysis for the staple, college and novelty lines. You might wish to develop further analyses for the staple and novelty lines based on the channel of distribution used.

No specific exercise was provided for the detailed self-analysis or internal marketing audit. If you are doing this in real time, then you should seek to answer the detailed questions suggested in Chapter 5 and use one of the planning texts such as Aubrey Wilson's *Marketing Audit Checklists* (1993) for guidance. For the purposes of the book you should seek to provide answers to the six general questions we posed:

1 What is the company's present position?
2 What is the company good at?
3 What are the major problems faced?
4 What is the company poor at?
5 What major resources, expertise exist?
6 What major resources, expertise deficiencies exist?

In addressing these questions James Barnstaple might have come up with a summary statement along the following lines:

Self-analysis

The immediate problem is that we have a large unsold inventory on two of our major product lines. This will have to be written off, resulting in a loss for the third year in a row. The worrying thing is that even if we'd sold these diaries we'd only have made a notional profit so the other eighty per cent of the business can't be doing very well either. Even more worrying is that my three functional managers aren't working as a team and can only see things from their own perspective. Worse still, the accountant is incompetent.

On the positive side, we have a fairly diversified customer base and are seen as diary specialists. This image/reputation is backed up with particular skills in printing and binding both pocket and desk-sized annual record systems. However, the barriers to entry for this business are low and I can think of several medium-sized jobbing printers who could make diaries as a seasonal line without having to face our inventory problems. Also, in the longer term, cheap, portable electronic diaries are a direct threat.

While some of the comments here may be opaque (e.g. the accountant is incompetent), your own analysis should have led you to this conclusion!

The four remaining exercises (5.7–5.10) are designed to help you synthesize the conclusions of your marketing appreciation into a single summary statement or SWOT analysis. For Barnstaple Company this might appear as follows:

Barnstaple SWOT

Strengths	Weaknesses

'Precision' printing
Multiple markets
Multiple distribution channels
    (i.e. established customer base)
	Lack of management skills – poor grasp
	    of business
	Seasonality
	Single product line

Opportunities	**Threats**

Business markets
    stationery
    business cards
Gift markets
    other paper-based record systems –
    address books, telephone numbers,
    etc.
	More efficient printers (short term)
	Electronic organizers (long term)

Chapter 6

The exercises in Chapter 6 are all designed to help answer the question: 'Where do we want to go?'. Many of these are straightforward analytical frameworks designed to help you organize and structure your own thinking. As such, again there are no 'right' answers. However, for purposes of comparison, Figure A2 shows James Barnstaple's solutions to the exercises.

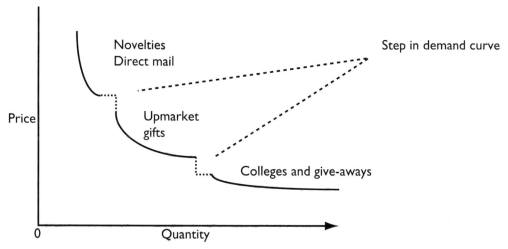

Figure A2 James Barnstaple's solutions to the exercises

Exercise 6.2 The product life cycle curve

Diaries are clearly in the mature/decline phase of the life cycle.

Exercise 6.3 Ansoff's growth/vector matrix

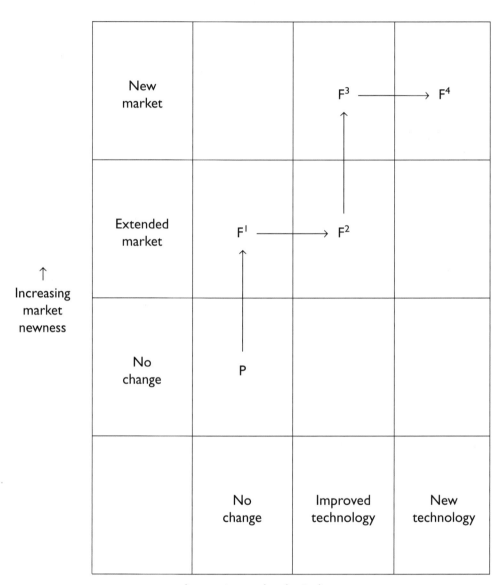

Increasing technological newness →

Barnstaple's strategic direction is based on the principles of economy, efficiency and effectiveness. In the short term (P) he must work with what he's got in terms of established customers and products. The first priority is to undertake a product line analysis so that he has a better understanding of where the costs and revenues occur with a view to reducing costs and improving revenues.

Earlier we offered the opinion that the accountant is incompetent. In reality it is unlikely that he is qualified and a plausible scenario is that he was a bookkeeper keeping a simple set of accounts for Mr Barnstaple Senior. In this privileged position he would know where the money was coming from and also, in a private company, where it was going! On Barnstaple Senior's death it was fairly predictable that his widow would ask the bookkeeper to take over running the company on a caretaker basis. From the evidence he doesn't appear to have much influence on the sales and production manager. If he had, why was the production manager allowed to make college diaries for stock against an illusory cost saving? (If you think about how diaries are sold, most would be sent out in September/October for sale/delivery in November/December. Goods produced in November/December would then have to be held in stock for up to a year with one exception – the college lines for January delivery. What Barnstaple could do with are more college accounts and firm orders for January delivery and manufacture in November/December!)

However, the charge of incompetence is based on the financial data presented, the assumptions underlying it and the interpretations made. What you need to do is a contribution analysis which indicates that the accountant's advice to drop both college and novelty lines will result in an immediate loss of contribution of £375,000 against allocated factory overheads of £375,000 and selling and administrative costs of £275,000. The sales manager's solution loses you £225,000 and the production manager's suggestion £150,000. Hardly the way to turn the company round!

You might also want to question the allocation of overheads to the two lines. While this is always an arbitrary matter it seems unreasonable that twelve college lines bear £125,000 selling and administrative expenses while 100 novelty lines only carry £25,000 more.

So what to do in the short term? Drop the novelty lines and save £312,500 of labour costs and £187,500 of material costs. Redeploy the sales effort to increasing the number of college accounts with two delivery dates. Third, from your analysis (we can't do this) of the staple lines, put more effort behind those with the biggest contribution.

As a result of our economy drive, we should become more efficient and consider extending our market with current products (F^1). Simultaneously we should look at the opportunities for new product development which builds upon our existing technology. What other paper-based, printed and bound products would appeal to our existing customer base which are not seasonal such as diaries? Telephone and address books, Visitor books, Notebooks, etc. (F^2).

By creating new products it becomes possible to enter new markets (F^3) and broaden our customer franchise.

Finally, (F^4) we might be able to leverage our customer franchise by becoming a value added reseller (VAR) for the electronics firms who we see as a long-term threat. If we do, we will have diversified (new products in new markets) and restored effectiveness.

Exercises 6.4, 6.5 and 6.6

We do not have enough information from the case data to complete these diagnostic frameworks. Given a more detailed case study or a real-world organization, the various boxes should improve your understanding of the various strategic moves available to you.

Exercise 6.7 Mission statement

James Barnstaple has a number of options open to him, and as the owner/manager can develop his mission statement around the alternatives which appeal to him most. Given earlier answers, an appropriate statement might be:

> To be a supplier of personal paper-based record systems calling for high-quality printing and binding skills.

Exercise 6.8 Setting objectives

Derived from this simple mission statement, Barnstaple's list of major objectives might appear as follows:

Directional objectives
1 To review all products on a regular basis and eliminate those with a small contribution.
2 To cease production of novelty lines for sale through jobbers.
3 To increase the number of college and corporate accounts.
4 To develop a range of non-seasonal gift and promotional products utilizing our existing skills and resources.

Performance objectives
1 To restore the company to profitability in the current year.
2 To increase the budgeted net profit from about 3.3 per cent by 1 per cent per annum for the next six years until it reaches 10 per cent per annum. (If you want to know where 3.3 per cent comes from, see the next exercise.)

Internal objectives
1 (Depending on age/motivation) To reskill (or replace) the functional managers.
2 To set up a product line analysis system.
3 To set up a marketing research information system.

External objectives
1 To build and strengthen relationships with the currently most profitable corporate customers.
2 To work closely with suppliers and customers to develop new 'non-seasonal' products.

Exercise 6.9 Stating assumptions

To exemplify the formulation of assumptions we will explain the comment on performance objective 2 in the previous exercise regarding profitability. This would not be an assumption for Mr Barnstaple as he would have the information; as case analysts we don't know but we can deduce what profitability is and then assume this to be a correct figure.

We are told that if the inventory had been sold apart from the usual inventory loss of £15,000, then 'a satisfactory profit' would have been earned. Well, if the inventory had been sold, then sales in the college and novelty lines would have been £1,562,000 and as these represent twenty per cent of turnover total sales would have been £7,810,000. But the lost profit from the unsold inventory is £275,000 less £15,000 normal loss = £260,000. From this it would seem that 'a satisfactory profit' would have been:

$$\frac{260,000}{7,810,000} = 3.3\%$$

While you could identify some issues about which Barnstaple might want to make assumptions, you really need more information than we have to do this effectively.

Exercise 6.11 Core strategy and approach

Barnstaple is committed to a differentiated strategy (he has two major product lines if he drops the novelties) and a combination of push and pull approaches, with an emphasis on the former. Concentrating on corporate accounts will involve personal selling and incentives to intermediaries to stock/buy the diaries. On the other hand, direct selling will call for media advertising to stimulate orders from end-users.

Exercises 6.12 and 6.13 Motivations/benefits sought

For these exercises we provided evidence from prior research concerning people's motivation for going on holiday and the benefits looked for. By now you should be familiar with the procedure for completing factor rating tables using the experts' rankings for the two exercises.

Exercise 6.12 Motives for going on holiday

Motive for holiday	Stage 1 – Individual ranking	Stage 2 – Team ranking	Stage 3 – Experts' ranking	Stage 4 – Difference between stages 1 and 3	Stage 5 – Difference between stages 2 and 3
a Eat well			12		
b Recover strength			13		
c Experience other countries			7		
d Get exercise, sports and games activities			5		
e Be with other people, have company			15		
f Experience a great deal, have diversity			6		
g Switch off, relax			1		
h Get away from everyday life			8		
i Experience something entirely different			9		
j Do as one pleases, be free			3		
k Cleaner air, cleaner water, get out of the polluted environment			14		
l Have time for one another			2		
m Get sunshine, escape bad weather			4		
n Have a lot of fun and entertainment			10		
o Experience nature			11		
				Total:	Total:

Exercise 6.13 Benefits sought when choosing holiday destinations

Benefit sought	Stage 1 – Individual ranking	Stage 2 – Team ranking	Stage 3 – Experts' ranking	Stage 4 – Difference between stages 1 and 3	Stage 5 – Difference between stages 2 and 3
a Festivals/folklore			18		
b Uncrowded/ peaceful			6		
c Family orientation			17		
d Unspoilt/ attractive environment			1		
e Fitness facilities			19		
f Value for money			12		
g Climate/weather			2		
h Picturesque-ness			3		
i Children's arrangements			15		
j Shopping facilities			16		
k Good restaurants			9		
l Good eating and drinking facilities			5		
m Friendly service			4		
n Sightseeing/ cultural life/ excursions			13		
o Recreational facilities			11		
p Entertainment facilities			14		
q Accommodation			8		
r Friendliness of locals			10		
s Accessibility			7		
				Total:	Total:

Exercise 6.14 (Segmentation performance appraisal) and
Exercise 6.15 (Positioning maps)

Completion of this analysis calls for specific product data which is lacking for Barnstaple (unless you've done some secondary research). However, if you are working on your own company you should have sufficient information to complete the exercises.

Chapter 7

Like the preceding two exercises, we really do not have enough data to come up with any kind of detailed analysis called for by most of these exercises. That said, you could speculate about user needs (Exercise 7.2) and have most of the information required for the product policy indication (Exercise 7.3); similarly, for Exercise 7.4 (NPD policies and performance), Exercise 7.8 (Developing a promotional plan), and Exercise 7.9 (Marketing mix summary). Given earlier analysis and decisions, your answers to these exercises should be self-evident.

For Exercise 7.3 we have inserted some notional scores on the proforma on page 221. The higher the score the better the indications.

Exercise 7.3 Product policy indications

At what stage of the PLC is the product? (introduction/growth/maturity/decline) ① ⑤ ③ ②	
What is the elasticity of demand? (elastic/unitary/inelastic) ⑤ ③ ①	
What is the current generic strategy? (undifferentiated/differentiated/ concentrated)	
What is your basic marketing approach? (push or pull)	
Which of Ansoff's strategies are you following? (penetration, product development, market development, diversification) (score 1 for each)	
Are your sales growing/stable/declining? ⑤ ③ ①	
Are there any close substitutes for your product? (score 5 for no; 1 for yes)	
How well does your product meet user needs? (excellent/good/fair/poor) ⑤ ③ ② ①	

Chapter 8

Exercise 8.1 Project planning and implementation

The expert rankings for this exercise are listed on the pro forma. As with other earlier exercises, these reflect the considered opinion of experts and it will be helpful if you rewrite the experts' answers in rank order, when the logic will be more apparent than it is in a jumbled sequence on the pro forma. Experience with this exercise indicates that individual deviations from the normative solution are largely a matter of ambiguity and semantics.

	Management activities	Step 1 – Individual ranking	Step 2 – Team ranking	Step 3 – Experts' ranking	Step 4 – Difference between steps 1 and 3	Step 5 – Difference between steps 2 and 3
1	**A** Establish milestones to assess progress			11		
2	**B** Make necessary adjustments to plan			23		
3	**C** Train personnel for new appointments			17		
4	**D** Identify possible courses of action			7		
5	**E** Establish current position			3		
6	**F** Define the problem to be addressed			1		
7	**G** Reward/correct/punish individual performance			24		
8	**H** Define acceptable variances from planned performance			12		
9	**I** Agree individual performance objectives			18		
10	**J** Estimate outcomes for each course of action			8		
11	**K** Collect additional data			5		
12	**L** Develop a strategy			10		
13	**M** Assign authority, responsibility and accountability			19		
14	**N** Specify the precise tasks to be performed			13		
15	**O** Set objectives			2		
16	**P** Appraise individual performance			22		
17	**Q** Select qualified personnel			16		
18	**R** State assumptions			6		
19	**S** Select preferred course of action			9		
20	**T** Initiate project			20		
21	**U** Determine additional information needs			4		
22	**V** Assess progress against agreed milestones/targets			21		
23	**W** Spell out desired organizational structure			14		
24	**X** Allocate resources			15		
	Totals (the lower the score the better)					
					Individual score Step 4	Team score Step 5

Exercise 8.2 Developing a critical path for a new product

The normative model of NPD proposed by Booz, Allen and Hamilton (1982) contains the following stages:

- Exploration or idea generation
- Screening or concept testing
- Business analysis
- Development
- Testing
- Commercialization.

Each of these steps may be disaggregated further if you wish and some writers distinguish twelve or more distinct phases. These form the critical path. How much detail you include is up to you. As the multiple convergent processing model illustrated in Figure 8.1 indicates, this can be very complex and may require several sheets of paper to complete.

Exercise 8.3 Measurement, feedback and control

There is no right answer to this exercise – it is another device to help you formalize your judgement and then make a structured analysis of how well the chosen measures meet your needs.

Extra copies of exercises

Exercise 3.1 What business are we in?

What is the basic need you serve?

What products/services do you sell?

What specific benefits do they offer?

Do your competitors sell other kinds of products or services? What are they?

What benefits do these other products offer?

How would you describe the customers you serve?

Exercise 3.2 How marketing orientated are you?

	Strongly agree	Agree	Disagree	Strongly disagree

IN MY ORGANIZATION:

1. The sales force is expected to sell what the factory can make. ☐ ☐ ☐ ☐

2. There is an emphasis on short-term profits at the expense of long-term success in the marketplace. ☐ ☐ ☐ ☐

3. We believe customers must get what they want, even if it is rather unprofitable for the company. ☐ ☐ ☐ ☐

4. The business is committed to a long-term strategic point of view, supported by thorough market planning. ☐ ☐ ☐ ☐

5. We focus primarily on the bottom line and productivity, and only then on the customer and the marketplace. ☐ ☐ ☐ ☐

6. Subjective sales-force forecasts largely determine the production process. ☐ ☐ ☐ ☐

7. We base the price of our products on cost only, worked out by the accountants, who dictate pricing strategy almost regardless of the marketplace. ☐ ☐ ☐ ☐

8. Research and engineering are the heart of the business and our marketing people are not usually involved in determining what products we should make. ☐ ☐ ☐ ☐

9. The factory floor is the focal centre of the organization. ☐ ☐ ☐ ☐

Continued

	Strongly agree	Agree	Disagree	Strongly disagree
10. Productivity improvements often result in changes to product specification which make the product difficult to sell to the customer.	☐	☐	☐	☐
11. Capital investment decisions which involve new technology and the relocation of manufacturing plant rarely involve the marketing people.	☐	☐	☐	☐
12. We believe that selling volume comes first. Profits then generally follow.	☐	☐	☐	☐
13. We believe in the principle of managing the marketplace, by expecting – and managing – change.	☐	☐	☐	☐
14. We tend to fit our forecasts to the profits that we know are expected of us; then we plan how to achieve the forecast.	☐	☐	☐	☐
15. We don't pay a lot of attention to market research.	☐	☐	☐	☐
16. Product planning takes place on the factory floor, not in the marketing department.	☐	☐	☐	☐
17. Product costs, consumer prices and the whole panoply of customer-service expenditure tends to be based on profit needs, not market needs.	☐	☐	☐	☐
18. We tend to see ourselves as manufacturers rather than as marketers.	☐	☐	☐	☐
19. Our R&D people don't spend much time talking to the sales and marketing people.	☐	☐	☐	☐

Continued

	Strongly agree	Agree	Disagree	Strongly disagree
20. If customers aren't happy with our products, we tend to go looking for new customers rather than new products.	☐	☐	☐	☐
21. We tend to be more concerned with return on investment in the short term, than with customer satisfaction in the long term.	☐	☐	☐	☐
22. Our focus is on the marketplace: identifying customer needs and meeting those needs – profitably.	☐	☐	☐	☐
23. Our sales people are given great freedom in pricing, servicing and credit terms.	☐	☐	☐	☐
24. The product is the concern of our technical people, with little input from the marketing people.	☐	☐	☐	☐
25. The emphasis is on a balance between market share, market status and long-term profitability.	☐	☐	☐	☐
26. Marketing guidance for the engineers and the production people is often weak or non-existent.	☐	☐	☐	☐
27. We work with a lot of information feedback systems from the marketplace to measure and guide our activities.	☐	☐	☐	☐
28. We tend to over-engineer our products way past the point of customer need – and his or her ability to pay.	☐	☐	☐	☐

Exercise 4.1 Competitive critical success factors

Product factors influencing competitiveness	Stage 1 – Individual ranking	Stage 2 – Team ranking	Stage 3 – Experts' ranking	Stage 4 – Difference between stages 1 and 3	Stage 5 – Difference between stages 2 and 3
a. Style/fashion					
b. Durability					
c. Flexibility and adaptability of the product in use					
d. Parts availability and cost					
e. Attractive appearance/shape					
f. Technical sophistication					
g. Performance in operation					
h. Ease of use					
i. Sale price					
j. Safety in use					
k. Reliability					
l. Ease of maintenance					
m. Quality of after-sales service					
n. Efficient delivery					
o. Advertising and promotion					
p. Operator comfort					
				Total	Total

Management factors influencing competitiveness	Stage 1 – Individual ranking	Stage 2 – Team ranking	Stage 3 – Experts' ranking	Stage 4 – Difference between stages 1 and 3	Stage 5 – Difference between stages 2 and 3
a. Willingness to enter into collaborative arrangements					
b. Readiness to carry out in-depth research before entering new markets					
c. Readiness to adopt modern techniques (e.g. CAD, CAM, FMS, robotization, quality circles, etc.)					
d. Readiness to look far ahead into the future					
e. Close co-operation between research and development, production and marketing					
f. Effective management of design and innovation					
g. Effective use of ideas derived from the market					
h. Effective use of ideas derived from technology					
i. Clear objectives					
j. Top management support					
k. Government support					
				Total	Total

Factors influencing the design and development of new products	Stage 1 – Individual ranking	Stage 2 – Team ranking	Stage 3 – Experts' ranking	Stage 4 – Difference between stages 1 and 3	Stage 5 – Difference between stages 2 and 3
a. The authority/power of the person directing a project					
b. The product has a higher technological content than rival product offerings					
c. Close interaction with customers/users during the stages of design and development					
d. Continuous product reviews during and after product design and development in the light of changes in the environment					
e. Extensive use of new and improved manufacturing techniques					
f. Product is designed and developed by a team of qualified engineering and industrial designers					
g. Designers see the product through to commercialization					
				Total	Total

Exercise 5.1 PEST analysis

Political factors	Economic factors
1	1
2	2
3	3
4	4
5	5
Social factors	**Technological factors**
1	1
2	2
3	3
4	4
5	5

Exercise 5.2 Cross-impact matrix

Event	Probability	1	2	3	4	5
1						
2						
3						
4						
5						

Exercise 5.3 Completing the ETOM

Factor		Event/issue (1)	T (–) (2)	O (+) (3)	Weighting (1–5) (4)	Importance (1–15) (5)	Impact on company strategy (6)
Economic	1						
	2						
	3						
	4						
	5						
Subtotal							
Social and cultural	1						
	2						
	3						
	4						
	5						
Subtotal							
Demographic	1						
	2						
	3						
	4						
	5						
Subtotal							
Geographic	1						
	2						
	3						
	4						
	5						
Subtotal							
Political	1						
	2						
	3						
	4						
	5						
Subtotal							
Government and legal	1						
	2						
	3						
	4						
	5						
Subtotal							
Technological	1						
	2						
	3						
	4						
	5						
Subtotal							
Competitive	1						
	2						
	3						
	4						
	5						
Subtotal							
						Total (–) (+)	

Summary of environmental threat and opportunity matrix

Participant	Summary of top three ranked environmental factors		
	Description	Opportunity (+)	Threat (−)
1	1 2 3		
2	1 2 3		
3	1 2 3		
4	1 2 3		
5	1 2 3		
6	1 2 3		
7	1 2 3		
8	1 2 3		
9	1 2 3		
10	1 2 3		
11	1 2 3		
12	1 2 3		
13	1 2 3		
14	1 2 3		
15	1 2 3		

Exercise 5.4 Critical success factors

Critical success factor	Weighting	Own Firm rating score	Competitor 1 rating score	Competitor 2 rating score	Competitor 3 rating score

Exercise 5.5 Skills and competences

Distinctive competence

Product/market

Production

Finance

Technology

Organization and human resources

Core competences

Exercise 5.6 Objective needs analysis

Product Factor	Rating					
	Excellent 5	Good 4	Average 3	Fair 2	Poor 1	Not applicable 0
Performance						
Reliability						
Price						
Availability/delivery						
Technical sophistication						
After-sales service						
Ease of use						
Safety						
Ease of maintenance						
Parts availability/cost						
Attractive appearance						
Others:						
Total						Overall total

Exercise 5.7 Macroenvironmental threat and opportunity matrix

Factor	Event/issue	Threat/ opportunity	Probability/ importance	Impact
Political	1 2 3 4 5			
Economic	1 2 3 4 5			
Social	1 2 3 4 5			
Technological	1 2 3 4 5			

Exercise 5.8 Task environment threat and opportunity matrix

Factor	Event/issue	Threat/ opportunity	Probability/ importance	Impact
Market	1 2 3 4 5			
Competitors	1 2 3 4 5			
Suppliers/ intermediaries	1 2 3 4 5			
Other value chain elements	1 2 3 4 5			

Exercise 5.9 Occurrence/impact matrix

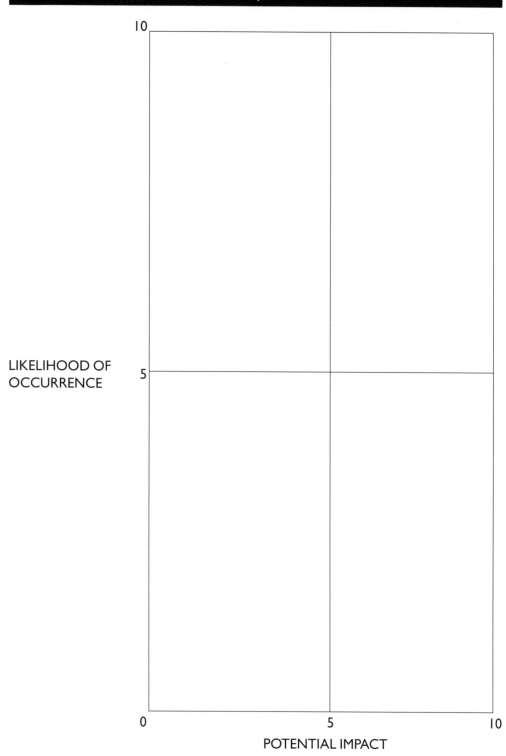

Exercise 5.10 SWOT analysis

STRENGTHS	OPPORTUNITIES
WEAKNESSES	THREATS

Exercise 6.1 The product demand curve

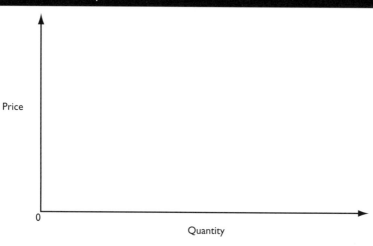

Exercise 6.2 The product life cycle curve

1 At what stage is the industry life cycle?

Embryonic

Growth

Mature

Decline

2 Draw the PLC for your product in the space below. Remember the key dimensions are output/sales over time.

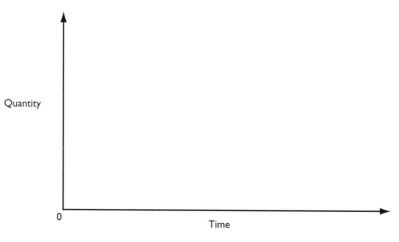

PLC for product

Exercise 6.3 Ansoff's growth/vector matrix

New market			
Extended market			
No change			
	No change	Improved technology	New technology

↑
Increasing
market
newness

Increasing technological newness →

Exercise 6.4 The directional policy matrix (DPM)

		Market		
		Unattractive	Average	Attractive
	Weak			
Product	Average			
	Strong			

Exercise 6.5 The Boston box

Relative competitive position
(Market share)

	HIGH	LOW

Annual market growth rate

HIGH

LOW

Exercise 6.6 Baker's box

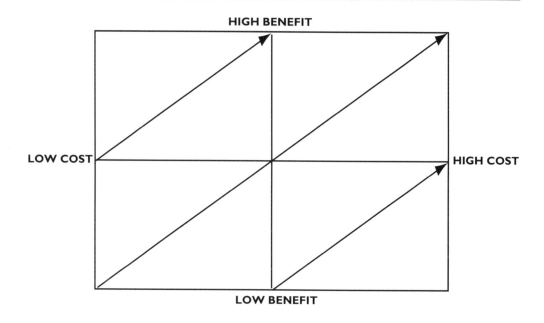

Exercise 6.7 Mission statement

Write in your mission statement here.

Exercise 6.8 Setting objectives

In the space below, list your major objectives:

Directional objectives

Performance objectives

Internal objectives

External objectives

Exercise 6.9 Stating assumptions

Write down your own list of critical issues/factors based on your marketing appreciation and your assumptions concerning them.

Issue/Factor

Assumption

Issue/Factor

Assumption

Issue/Factor

Assumption

Issue/Factor

Assumption

Issue/Factor

Assumption

Issue/Factor

Assumption

Exercise 6.10 Selecting a core strategy

Based on these definitions, you should now select your core strategy and write in a short statement justifying your selection.

We intend to follow a strategy of _____ because:

Exercise 6.11 Core strategy and approach

Product group	Alternatives			Approach	
	Undifferentiated	Differentiated	Concentrated	Push	Pull

Exercise 6.12 Motives for going on holiday

Motive for holiday	Stage 1 – Individual ranking	Stage 2 – Team ranking	Stage 3 – Experts' ranking	Stage 4 – Difference between stages 1 and 3	Stage 5 – Difference between stages 2 and 3
a Eat well					
b Recover strength					
c Experience other countries					
d Get exercise, sports and games activities					
e Be with other people, have company					
f Experience a great deal, have diversity					
g Switch off, relax					
h Get away from everyday life					
i Experience something entirely different					
j Do as one pleases, be free					
k Cleaner air, cleaner water, get out of the polluted environment					
l Have time for one another					
m Get sunshine, escape bad weather					
n Have a lot of fun and entertainment					
o Experience nature					
				Total:	Total:

Exercise 6.13 Benefits sought when choosing holiday destinations

Benefit sought	Stage 1 – Individual ranking	Stage 2 – Team ranking	Stage 3 – Experts' ranking	Stage 4 – Difference between stages 1 and 3	Stage 5 – Difference between stages 2 and 3
a Festivals/folklore					
b Uncrowded/ peaceful					
c Family orientation					
d Unspoilt/ attractive environment					
e Fitness facilities					
f Value for money					
g Climate/weather					
h Picturesque-ness					
i Children's arrangements					
j Shopping facilities					
k Good restaurants					
l Good eating and drinking facilities					
m Friendly service					
n Sightseeing/ cultural life/ excursions					
o Recreational facilities					
p Entertainment facilities					
q Accommodation					
r Friendliness of locals					
s Accessibility					
				Total:	Total:

Exercise 6.14 Segmentation performance appraisal

Product:

Segmentation factor	Weighting	Performance						Score
		1	2	3	4	5	N/A	

Exercise 6.15 Positioning maps

Exercise 7.1 Current status

Product sales

By product

Product/ service	Sales				
	19–	19–	19–	19–	19–

By geographical area

Product/service

Area	Sales				
	19–	19–	19–	19–	19–

By market segment

Product/service

Area	Sales				
	19–	19–	19–	19–	19–

Product uses

Product/ service	Major uses	Target market (for major uses)	Subsidiary uses	Target market (for subsidiary uses)
1				
2				
3				
4				

Substitute products

Product/service
(Fill in a form for each product/service in your portfolio)

Substitute product(s)	Producing company	Similarities	Differences	Advantages	Disadvantages
		(of substitute product compared to your product)			

Exercise 7.2 User needs

Product/service

Target market

Column 1 Need element	Column 2 Need intensity	Column 3 Need stability	Column 4 Need diffusion

Exercise 7.3 Product policy indications

At what stage of the PLC is the product? (introduction/growth/maturity/decline)	
What is the elasticity of demand? (elastic/unitary/inelastic)	
What is the current generic strategy? (undifferentiated/differentiated/ concentrated)	
What is your basic marketing approach? (push or pull)	
Which of Ansoff's strategies are you following? (penetration, product development, market development, diversification)	
Are your sales growing/stable/declining?	
Are there any close substitutes for your product?	
How well does your product meet user needs? (excellent/good/fair/poor)	

Exercise 7.4 NPD policies and performance

1 What percentage of your current sales is derived from products introduced:

in the past year   _____%

in the past five years   _____%

2 What percentage of your future sales will come from new products:

next year   _____%

next five years   _____%

3 Do you have a formal policy for NPD?

_____YES

_____NO

4 Which of the following approaches to NPD do you use? (Tick all that apply):

New product committee   ☐

Venture team   ☐

New product department   ☐

Product managers   ☐

5 Where do your ideas for new products come from?

Customers   ☐

Suppliers   ☐

R&D   ☐

Production   ☐

Marketing   ☐

Other   ☐

Exercise 7.5 Current service offerings

Product/service

Target market

	Current service
Pre-transaction	
Transaction	
Post-transaction	

- Comparing this with the results from Exercise 7.2, do you think there are any areas where the current service provision is deficient?

Exercise 7.6 Pricing policy and methods

1 What are the key issues influencing your pricing decision?

2 What is your pricing objective(s)? Why?

3 How important is price in your marketing mix? Why? (Remember the demand curve and price elasticity)

4 What basic strategy – skimming or penetration – do you follow? Why?

5 To what extent are your pricing methods influenced by cost, by demand, by competition? What is the relative influence of these three forces?

6 What is your preferred pricing method? Why?

Exercise 7.7 Distribution policy

Channel consideration	Description	Indicated channel length	
		L	S
Market or customer characteristics 　1 Size of purchasing unit 　2 Number of customers 　3 Location of customers 　4 Customer knowledge 　5 Installation and servicing 　　assistance			
Producer characteristics 　1 Size of firm 　2 Length of time in business 　3 Financial resources 　4 Location to the market 　5 Control over marketing programme 　6 Overall resource position 　7 Market coverage desired 　8 Managerial capabilities 　9 Market information availability 10 Power 11 Policy toward pushing product			
Environmental characteristics 　1 Number of competitors 　2 Number of resources controlled 　3 Economic conditions 　4 Entry and exit of producers 　5 Economic customs and traditions 　6 Location of competitors 　7 Laws and regulations 　8 Competition among customers 　9 Market to be served			
Product characteristics 　1 Perishability 　2 Fashionability 　3 Size of product 　4 Value of product			

Channel consideration	Description	Indicate channel len	
		L	S

5 Weight of product
6 Complexity of product
  a Special knowledge for sale
  b Installation
  c Maintenance
  d Service
7 Risk of obsolescence
8 Age of product
9 Production process
10 Order size (quantities purchased)
11 Appearance of product
12 Type of product (buying characteristics)
13 Type of product (market)
14 Time of purchase
15 Timing of purchase
16 Regularity of purchase
17 Profit margin
18 Width of product line
19 Availability of requirements
20 Number of products per line
21 Product lines
22 Number of alternative uses			

Channel length analysis indicates we should choose:

1 Long channel   ☐
2 Short channel   ☐

Our proposed distribution strategy is:

A Exclusive   ☐
B Selective   ☐
C Intensive   ☐

Our reasons for this are:

Exercise 7.8 Developing a promotional plan

1 What is our promotional objective(s)?
2 How do we intend to measure achievement of the objective?
3 What appropriation/budget is available?
4 What do we want to tell the target audience?
5 How do we propose to tell them, i.e. what vehicle or media do we intend using? What proportion of the budget will be spent on each?
6 What measures will we use to assess effectiveness of the various media?

Exercise 7.9 Marketing mix summary

Product:	
Target market:	
Positioning statement:	

Stage in PLC:	Intro ☐	Growth ☐	Maturity ☐	Decline ☐

Core strategy:	Undifferentiated ☐	Differentiated ☐	Concentrated ☐

Key approach:	Push ___%	Pull ___%

Pricing:	Skimming ☐	Penetration ☐

Distribution:	Exclusive ☐	Selective ☐	Intensive ☐

Promotion:	Impersonal ___%	Personal ___%

Exercise 7.10 How well are we doing?

1 **Product policy**
   Overall, our management of product policy is:

Excellent	Very Good	Good	Average	Poor	Don't Know
☐	☐	☐	☐	☐	☐

2 **New product policy**
   Overall, our management of new product policy is:

Excellent	Very Good	Good	Average	Poor	Don't Know
☐	☐	☐	☐	☐	☐

3 **Service policy**
   Overall, our management of service policy is:

Excellent	Very Good	Good	Average	Poor	Don't Know
☐	☐	☐	☐	☐	☐

4 **Pricing policy**
   Overall, our management of pricing policy is:

Excellent	Very Good	Good	Average	Poor	Don't Know
☐	☐	☐	☐	☐	☐

5 **Promotional policy**
   Overall, our management of promotional policy is:

Excellent	Very Good	Good	Average	Poor	Don't Know
☐	☐	☐	☐	☐	☐

6 **Distribution policy**
   Overall, our management of distribution policy is:

Excellent	Very Good	Good	Average	Poor	Don't Know
☐	☐	☐	☐	☐	☐

Exercise 8.1 Project planning and implementation

Management activities	Step 1 – Individual ranking	Step 2 – Team ranking	Step 3 – Experts' ranking	Step 4 – Difference between steps 1 and 3	Step 5 – Difference between steps 2 and 3
A Establish milestones to assess progress					
B Make necessary adjustments to plan					
C Train personnel for new appointments					
D Identify possible courses of action					
E Establish current position					
F Define the problem to be addressed					
G Reward/correct/punish individual performance					
H Define acceptable variances from planned performance					
I Agree individual performance objectives					
J Estimate outcomes for each course of action					
K Collect additional data					
L Develop a strategy					
M Assign authority, responsibility and accountability					
N Specify the precise tasks to be performed					
O Set objectives					
P Appraise individual performance					
Q Select qualified personnel					
R State assumptions					
S Select preferred course of action					
T Initiate project					
U Determine additional information needs					
V Assess progress against agreed milestones/targets					
W Spell out desired organizational structure					
X Allocate resources					
Totals (the lower the score the better)					
				Individual score Step 4	Team score Step 5

Exercise 8.2 Developing a critical path for a new product

1 List the key events, activities and resources involved:

2 Order your list chronologically with timings and start and finish requirements:

Factor	Time required	Start	Finish

3 Plot your data as a critical path:

Exercise 8.3 Measurement, feedback and control

Activity	1 Priority			2 Competence					
	High	Med	Low	Very competent					Very incompetent
(a) Planning/Product									
1 Long-term (3+ years) review of *current markets*	I	I	0	I	2	3	4	5	6
2 Long-term review of *current products* (major money-spinners)	I	I	0	I	2	3	4	5	6
3 New product-developing market plans	I	I	0	I	2	3	4	5	6
4 Long-term review of *potential* new markets/products	I	I	0	I	2	3	4	5	6
5 Annual marketing plan for all major products/ranges	I	I	0	I	2	3	4	5	6
(b) Price–Costs									
6 Systematic competitor price monitoring	I	I	0	I	2	3	4	5	6
7 Cost monitoring (routine value analysis?)	I	I	0	I	2	3	4	5	6
8 Systematic price–cost–profit control	I	I	0	I	2	3	4	5	6
9 Systematic monitoring of discounts given to customers	I	I	0	I	2	3	4	5	6
(c) Selling									
10 Annual review of salesforce/selling strategy	I	I	0	I	2	3	4	5	6
11 Systematic and detailed sales order analysis	I	I	0	I	2	3	4	5	6
12 Annual 'Key Account' customer reviews	I	I	0	I	2	3	4	5	6
13 Cost-effectiveness analysis of customers called on	I	I	0	I	2	3	4	5	6
14 Control mechanisms on 'special' discounts	I	I	0	I	2	3	4	5	6
15 Annual review of salesforce's selling aids	I	I	0	I	2	3	4	5	6
(d) Promotion									
16 Annual planning of all promotional activities: advertising, PR, exhibitions, mail shots, etc.	I	I	0	I	2	3	4	5	6
17 Routine monitoring of competitor's promotional activity	I	I	0	I	2	3	4	5	6
18 Routine monitoring of promotional expenditure budgets	I	I	0	I	2	3	4	5	6
19 Ad agency/PR agency review systems	I	I	0	I	2	3	4	5	6
(e) Distribution/Channels									
20 Annual analysis of physical distribution effectiveness	I	I	0	I	2	3	4	5	6
21 Regular cost analysis of distribution service levels (guaranteed delivery time of routine orders, damaged stock policy, etc.)	I	I	0	I	2	3	4	5	6
22 Distribution (agent, retailer, wholesaler) effectiveness monitoring: pricing, display, stock levels, product range carried, etc.	I	I	0	I	2	3	4	5	6
23 Debtor-control systems	I	I	0	I	2	3	4	5	6
24 Credit-rating systems	I	I	0	I	2	3	4	5	6

Activity	1 Priority			2 Competence					
	High	Med	Low	Very competent					Very incompetent
(f) Market information									
25 Product acceptability data from end-user. Your products *and* your competitors	I	I	0	I	2	3	4	5	6
26 Market profiles of end-users (demographics, etc.)	I	I	0	I	2	3	4	5	6
27 Regular sales (volume and value) information for total market and market segments (annually, quarterly *or* monthly)	I	I	0	I	2	3	4	5	6
(g) Revenue management									
28 Routine review (monthly?) of progress of revenue and profits, product (range) by product	I	I	0	I	2	3	4	5	6

References

Alreck, P. and Settle, R. B. (1985) *The Survey Research Handbook* (Homewood, Illinois: Irwin)

Ansoff, H. I. (1968) *Corporate Strategy* (Harmondsworth: Pelican)

Baker, M. J. (1991) *Research for Marketing* (London: Macmillan)

Baker, M. J. (1992) *Marketing Strategy and Management*, 2nd edn (Basingstoke: Macmillan)

Baker, M. J. (1994) *The Marketing Book*, 3rd edn (Oxford: Butterworth-Heinemann)

Baker, M. J. (1996) *Marketing: An Introductory Text*, 6th edn (Basingstoke: Macmillan)

Baker, M. J. (ed.) (1995a) *Companion Encyclopedia of Marketing* (London: Routledge)

Baker, M. J. (ed.) (1995b) *Marketing: Theory and Practice*, 3rd edn (London: Macmillan)

Baker, M. J. and Hart, S. J. (1989) *Marketing and Competitive Success* (London: Philip Allan)

Bell, M. (1972) *Marketing: Concepts and Strategy*, 2nd edn (Boston, Mass.: Houghton Mifflin)

Booz-Allen and Hamilton, (1982) *New Products Management for the 1980s* (New York: Booz-Allen and Hamilton)

Brady, D. L. (1978) *An Analysis of Factors Affecting the Methods of Exporting Used by Small Manufacturing Firms* (University of Alabama)

Brownlie, D. (1983) Chapter 11 in *Marketing: Theory and Practice*, edited by Michael J. Baker (London: Macmillan)

Brownlie, D. (1994) Chapter 7 in *The Marketing Book*, 3rd edn, edited by Michael J. Baker (Oxford: Butterworth-Heinemann)

Business International Corporation (1986) *A Guide to Corporate Survival and Growth, The New Thinking* (New York: BIC)

Carsberg, B. (1975) *Economics of Business Decisions* (Harmondsworth: Penguin)

Chandler, A. D. (1962) *Strategy and Structure* (Cambridge, Mass.: MIT Press)

Clarkson, T. (1996) *Course Notes MTM Programme* (Heriot-Watt and Strathclyde Universities)

Crosier, K. (1975) What exactly is marketing? *Quarterly Review of Marketing*, Winter

Crosier, K. (1994) Chapter 19 in *The Marketing Book*, 3rd edn, edited by Michael J. Baker (Oxford: Butterworth-Heinemann)

Crosier, K. (1995) Chapter 6 in *Marketing: Theory and Practice*, 3rd edn, edited by Michael J. Baker (London: Macmillan)

Day, G. S. and Wensley, R. (1988) Assessing advantage: a framework for diagnosing competitive superiority, *Journal of Marketing*, **52**(2), April, 1–20

Doyle, P. (1994) 'Branding', Chapter 20 in *The Marketing Book*, 3rd edn, edited by Michael J. Baker (Oxford: Butterworth-Heinemann)

Drucker, P. F. (1954) *The Practice of Management* (New York: Harper & Row)

Evans, J. R. and Berman, B. (1982) *Marketing Management* (Macmillan)

Fisher, L. (1966) *Industrial Marketing* (London: Business Books)

Gaedeke, R. M. and Tootelian, D. (1983) *Marketing: principles and application* (St. Paul, Minnesota: West Publishing Co.)

Goodwin, P. and Wright, G. (1991) *Decision Analysis for Management Judgement* (Chichester: Wiley)

Goslin, Lewis, N. (1967) *The Product Planning System* (Homewood, Illinois: Richard D. Irwin Inc.)

Green, P. E. and Tull, D. S. (1978) *Research for Marketing Decisions*, 4th edn (Englewood Cliffs, N. J.: Prentice-Hall)

Greene, M. R. (1969) How to rationalize your marketing risks, *Harvard Business Review*, May–June

Greenley, G. (1986) *The Strategic and Operational Planning of Marketing* (McGraw-Hill)

Hammond III, J. S. (1967) Better decisions with preference theory, *Harvard Business Review*, November–December

Hart, S. and Baker, M. J. (1994) Multiple convergent processing, *International Marketing Review*, 11(1), 77–92

Hutt, M. D. and Speh, T. W. (1995) *Business Marketing Management* (Dryden Press)

Jackson, K. F. (1977) *The Art of Solving Problems* (London: Teach Yourself Books)

Jain, S. C. (1990) *Marketing Planning and Strategy*, 3rd edn (Cincinnati, Ohio: South-Western)

Johnson, S. C. and Jones, C. (1957) How to organize for new products, *Harvard Business Review*, May–June

Klemm, Mary et al (1991) Selling corporate values to employees, *Long Range Planning*

Kotler, P. (1988) *Marketing Management: Analysis, Planning, Implementation and Control*, 6th edn (Englewood Cliffs, N. J.: Prentice-Hall)

Krippendorf, J. (1987) *The Holiday Makers* (Oxford: Butterworth-Heinemann)

Levitt, T. (1960) Marketing myopia, *Harvard Business Review,* July–August

Levitt, T. (1983) *The Marketing Imagination* (New York: Free Press)

Magee, J. F. (1964) Decision trees for decision making, *Harvard Business Review,* July–August

Martin, P. and Bateson, P. (1986) *Measuring Behaviour* (Cambridge: Cambridge University Press)

McIntosh, R. W. and Goeldner, C. R. (1990) *Tourism: Principles, Practices, Philosophies,* 6th edition (New Jersey: Wiley)

McKay, E. S, (1972) *The Marketing Mystique* (New York: The American Management Association)

Meadows, D. L. and Meadows, D. H. (1972) *Limits to Growth* (Signet)

Middleton, V. T. C. (1994) *Marketing in Travel and Tourism,* 2nd edn (Oxford: Butterworth-Heinemann)

Mintzberg, H. and Walters, J. A. (1985) Of strategies, deliberate and emergent, *Strategic Management Journal,* **6,** 257–272

Moore, P. G. and Thomas, H. (1976) *The Anatomy of Decisions* (Harmondsworth: Penguin)

Moser, C. A. and Kalton, G. (1971) *Survey Methods in Social Investigation,* 2nd edn (Heinemann)

Murphy, P. E. (1985) *Tourism: A Community Approach* (New York: Methuen)

Nanus, B. (1982) QUEST – Quick Environmental Scanning Technique, *Long Range Planning,* **15**(2), 39–45

O'Shaughnessy, J. (1984) *Competitive Marketing: A Strategic Approach* (Winchester, Mass.: Allen & Unwin)

Osgood, C. et al (1952) *Method and Theory in Experimental Psychology* (New York: Oxford University Press)

Porter, M. (1980) *Competitive Strategy: Techniques for Analyzing Industries and Competitors* (New York: Free Press)

Porter, M. (1985) *Competitive Advantage* (New York: Free Press)

Porter, M. (1990) *The Competitive Advantage of Nations* (London: Macmillan)

Pralahad, C. K. and Hamel, G. (1990) The core competence of the corporation, *Harvard Business Review,* May-June, 79–91

Robinson, P. J. and Luck, D. J. (1964) *Promotional Decision Making Practice and Theory,* Marketing Science Institute series (New York: McGraw-Hill)

Robinson, P. J., Faris, C. W. and Wind, Y. (1967) *Industrial Marketing and Creative Buying* (Boston: Allyn & Bacon)

Rothwell, R., Gardiner, P. and Schott, K. (1983) *Design and the Economy* (London: The Design Council)

Schedule Jr, P. A. (1964) POI for new product planning, *Harvard Business Review,* November–December

Schuchman, A. (1959) 'The Marketing Audit: Its nature, purposes and problems', *Analyzing and Improving Marketing Performance,* Report No. 32 (New York: American Management Association)

Smith, V. (1977) *Hosts and Guests: The Anthopology of Tourism* (University of Pennsylvania Press)

Teare, R. (1994) *Marketing in Hospitality and Tourism* (Cassell)

Toffler, A. (1972) *Future Shock* (Pan)

Tull, D. S. and Albaum, G. S. (1975) *Survey Research: A Decisional Approach* (Intertext Books)

Wilson, A. (1995) The marketing audit, Chapter 21 in *Encyclopedia of Marketing*, edited by Michael J. Baker (London: Routledge)

Wilson, R. M. S. and Gilligan, C. (1997) *Strategic Marketing Management*, 2nd edn (Oxford: Butterworth-Heinemann)

Witt, S. F. and Moutinho, L. (1994) *Tourism Marketing and Management Handbook*, 2nd edn (Prentice Hall)

Working Group on Joint Planning (1985) *Progress in Partnership* (Working Group on Joint Planning)

Index